The Spirit of Creativity

The Spirit of Creativity

Thoughts On Living One's Creative Truth

Joseph Curiale

The Spirit of Creativity

Orchard Road Music
PO Box 1545
Agoura Hills, CA 91376
Copyright ©2006 Joseph Curiale
All rights reserved.

Library of Congress Control Number: 2005910295
ISBN: Hardcover   1-4257-0322-4
               Softcover   1-4257-0321-6

Cover photograph and design: Joseph Curiale
Graphic design: Jeribai at New Creation Studio

The poem, "Being I" ©1995 Joseph Curiale

This book was printed in the United States of America.

To order additional copies of this book, contact:
Xlibris Corporation
1-888-795-4274
www.Xlibris.com
Orders@Xlibris.com
30740

*This book is gratefully dedicated to
all those who have been an inspiration to
the spirit of my creativity.*

Acknowledgements

In order to properly acknowledge everyone who played some kind of important role in my life, that ultimately lead to the inspiration and knowledge required to write this book, it would require a voluminous book itself that begins from birth. In light of this space/time reality, I would like to acknowledge those who were directly involved in kindly taking the time to read through the various drafts of the original manuscript, honestly sharing their thoughts with me: Peggy Ames, Chyla Anderson, Mr. Albert Andon, Steve and Sharon Binder, Dr. Elena Bonn, Yuriko Byers, Erin Collins, Bill Green, Paul Hosford, Chris Kohtz, Mark Lewis, Elizabeth Nelson, Stephen Pouliot, Susan Russel, Marlene Simon, and Ruth Lara Vichules. I realize that it's a tall order to ask people in this increasingly hectic world to find the time to read through a manuscript, so I'm all the more grateful to those who shared their time, thoughts, and friendship in a spirit of generosity, kindness, and caring. I gratefully thank all of you from the bottom of my heart.

I wish to thank the following people for kindly helping me to obtain permission to quote various authors: Michael and Justine Toms, and Bec Kageyama of New Dimensions Radio, Dr. Masaru Emoto and Kimiko Miyazawa, H.J. Witteveen, Jenell Forschler of Shambhala Publications, Inc., Lisa M. LaPointe and *The Journal of Creative Behavior*, and Gary Zukav.

I would like to extend my very special thanks to Elizabeth Nelson for sharing her expertise, helping to make the manuscript much better and more effective than it would have otherwise been. Thank you Elizabeth. And I would also like to give special thanks to Peggy Ames, for generously sharing her time reading through the various incarnations of the book, encouraging me to see it through to its full realization. It meant a lot. Thank you Peggy.

Chris Kohtz . . . You're a poet and a healer. You bring beautiful music to the world. Your aesthetic vision and insights have uplifted humanity, and the fruits of your goodness will reverberate forever.

Mr. Steve Binder . . . You are one of the kindest, sweetest and most caring people on this planet. Your friendship is a treasure that is incalculable. Your loving spirit is so much a part of my life and has so often lifted me up. Thank you for being an inextinguishable light in this world.

And Bill Green . . . How could I ever find the words that could possibly express the depth of gratitude, love, and appreciation I feel for all you have done in my behalf? You certainly have been the champion of champions for me and without you in my life this book and the music of my soul might have never come into existence. Our collaboration has been at the foundation of my creative unfolding, which has enriched all aspects of my life beyond measure. Your creative brilliance most certainly has allowed me to truly live. Thank you.

Once again, my sincere thankfulness to all of you for playing your own special part in the grand orchestration of this book's creation, adding to the love, goodness, and understanding that I hope it brings to the world.

Contents

"The creative person in a sense does something
for all of us simply by being,
and perhaps we help ourselves when we help such persons
in the process of their creative unfolding."

Frank Barron

Creative Person and the Creative Process

Introduction

Love helps us to endure the brutality of the world we live in. Creativity does too, perhaps because in its finest and most perfect form, creativity *is* love. It would be misleading and a distortion of the truth to paint an overly romantic view of the seeming nature of the universe. Our universe is one of great beauty and creativity, and yet at the same time one of brutal violence, ugliness and destruction. The physical universe we experience in this third dimension appears to be solid and also one where opposite polarities run the show. With that illusion as a basis, whether we like it or not, love cannot exist without hate. Light cannot exist without darkness. Pleasure cannot exist without pain. The hero cannot exist without a villain. I cannot say I'm very happy with this arrangement or approve of it, but it does *appear* to be the one in place. Yet the fact that I can imagine something better, a more loving universe without the ugliness and cruelty, leads me to believe it is within my personal power to create it both in a microcosmic way while I'm here, and in a larger way in the other worlds, dimensions, or wherever it is we are going.

Why must I accept the universe and this system on Earth as it is? I have said many times before, "Just because something *is,* doesn't mean that it should *be.*" If love is the fabric of the universe, the powerful force within an atom and, according to the Upanishads, "I Am That" (Tat Tvam Asi), then I *do* have the power to change the world. It is then within my power to do *anything* I can imagine. Imagination is the key to creativity and the key to creating a better and more beautiful world, a more loving world. The time frame is another story, but in the scheme of eternity, why should I be so concerned about time anyway? All that I should be concerned about is living my life in this moment with awareness and truth, with honesty and integrity, with love and creativity.

Joseph Curiale

What is Creativity?

Chapter One
What is Creativity?

"In order to create there must be a dynamic force,
and what force is more potent than love?"

Igor Stravinsky
Russian-born composer

If we believe that this very short lifetime is all that there is, it's easy to understand why we could feel substantial pressure to accomplish something as quickly as possible, something thought of as significant, in the hope of being validated by the world. We seem to be driven to immortalize ourselves, perhaps because there is something that feels so unnatural about dying. It seems so final. The thought of having lived and yet not having left a legacy of some kind can cause us to feel hurt, insignificant, or forgotten. It can make us feel like our life is meaningless, keeping us wondering what the point of it is, since so much of life seems to be such a struggle. But it is at the crossroad between life and death that we are given the opportunity to open our hearts and minds to a different reality. These reassuring words of Indian poet and Nobel Laureate Rabindranath Tagore give us a glimpse of that different reality: "Death is not extinguishing the light; it is only putting out the lamp because the Dawn has come."[1] We really *don't* die. One of the important ways we live on is through the spirit of our creativity. But what exactly is creativity?

Creativity is defined by one source as "the ability to use the imagination to develop new and original ideas or things, especially in an artistic context."[2] Another source defines it as "the ability to transcend traditional ideas, rules, patterns, relationships, to create meaningful new ideas, forms, methods, interpretations."[3] And to "create" is "to bring into existence."[4] But what compels us to create and why does it matter? What is the source, the power, the driving force behind creativity?

The need to create is as fundamental to our survival as is the water and air we need to live. Physiologically, when our bodies cease to create what they need to sustain life, they die. And since the mind and body are inseparably connected and increasingly referred to as the "bodymind," when we cease to create emotionally and artistically as well, our fate is the same, although we experience a much slower and more painful demise. Unfortunately, many people die emotionally, spiritually, and creatively long before they die physically because they have somehow failed to realize and express their unique creative gifts that are crucial to living a balanced, healthy life. But as long as we have life in us, we have the opportunity to live our creative truth.

We appear to be distinctly separate individuals with different shapes, sizes, and circumstances, but in reality, we are all part of a greater wholeness or "oneness." This is discussed in greater detail in *The Holographic Universe* by Michael Talbot[5], which explores the research of the late University of London quantum physicist, author, and protégé of Einstein, David Bohm, and Stanford University neurophysiologist and author, Karl Pribram who, unaware of each other's work, had come to the same conclusion at nearly the same time about the holographic nature of the universe and the brain. According to Michael Talbot, "Our brains mathematically construct reality by interpreting frequencies that are ultimately projections from another dimension, a deeper order of existence that is beyond both space and time: The brain is a hologram enfolded in a holographic universe."[6]

It is believed that the universe is expanding and in a continual state of creation. And since, under the holographic model of the universe, each of us contains the "whole," we don't actually have to *try* to be creative, we are *by nature* creative and creating all the time in one form or another. To better understand this holographic nature of the universe we can look to a hologram as a model. A hologram is a laser-generated image with three-dimensional properties that can be discerned from many viewpoints. If, however, the holographic film that was used to create the image is divided into many pieces, and a laser is projected through even the smallest fragment, the whole picture still remains, not only in that tiny piece, but also in *every piece*. The whole exists within the whole. The same is said to be true of us as part of the holographic universe. We are an inseparable part of the infinite creative whole we call God, Love, our Higher Power, Cosmic Mind,[7] Cosmic Consciousness, The Universe, Divine Love, The Ground of Being,[8] or any number of other ways, including the scientifically poetic, The Unified Field[9] (also known as the *Theory of Everything*), The Non-Local Field of Information with Self Referral Cybernetic Feedback Loops,[10] or one of my favorites of this type, The Undifferentiated Aesthetic Continuum.[11] And, if "God is love"[12] and love is the fabric of the universe, then love is the epitome of creativity: limitless, boundless, and infinite in its diversity. However, the beautiful light that must shine through us in order to realize this perfect wholeness is not a laser, it is the light of love that allows us to unlock our infinite creativity.

And so, if the universe is infinitely creative, and in a constant state of creation, *so are we*. We *are* that creativity. We *are* the love that we aspire to be and we must understand that it is not found outside of ourselves but is our own true nature. We connect with that infinite whole by referring back to the Divinity within ourselves, knowing, as mentioned in the Introduction, that *we are that* and that the Divine love within us *is* the power, the light, the driving force behind creativity. A variety of truly amazing life experiences, which I will touch upon throughout this book, have led me to believe in the holographic model that makes the seemingly inexplicable nature of things easier to understand: synchronicities, and a connectedness with all of creation when there appears to be no logical reason.

I am a composer of music, and although by the early 1990s I was enjoying much success as a composer and producer of music in Hollywood, Europe and Asia, I had come to crossroads both personally and professionally. I was living the life I had previously dreamed of, writing music for film, television, and recordings. And having been a staff writer for Columbia Pictures, a composer for the Tonight Show with Johnny Carson, and a freelance, I had the opportunity to work with so many of the icons of Hollywood. But I had gotten tired of the drudgery of working in commercial music. Early on it had been very exciting, but that excitement wore off surprisingly fast for me. The times were changing, and the quality and content of popular music was rapidly declining to a place that I felt had sunk far below where my integrity would allow me to go, not only as a musician, but also as a human being. Plus I saw the writing on the wall that there were going to be fewer and fewer opportunities for me in film, TV, and popular music, because my sensitive moral conscience would not allow me to go the way where popular trends were dragging music and entertainment. I was craving new creative experiences, more spiritually elevated experiences in music. A relentless restlessness grew in me, urging me on to dig deeper within myself and reach far beyond anything I had previously known or experienced in music and the arts. Looking back it all makes sense. The progression was a natural consequence that arose simultaneously with the evolution of my spiritual growth. My needs were changing. My values were changing too. The kind of work I was doing, and many of the other things that I had previously held so important, no longer carried any weight with me. Despite my being very grateful for all the wonderfully exciting and iconic experiences, and where they had gotten me, it was time to move on. That was a bit of a tough reality to face, when to "move on" meant upsetting the comfortably familiar status quo in my life. But things had gotten to the point where it didn't matter anymore; there was really no other sound choice but to change and grow.

I could no longer get away from the fact that the deep desire to write and record music without the limiting parameters set upon composers of commercial music was getting stronger in me day by day. I couldn't sweep those feelings under the rug anymore. It felt paramount to my sanity and my being able to continue living in my skin, to follow what the Divinity in my soul was guiding me to do. But I was so locked into the mindset and lifestyle of a commercial "blue collar" composer, feeding the ravenous lifestyle that comes along with the financial rewards such work can generate, that I felt I hadn't the peace of mind, a quiet mind, to be able to hear the music of my soul, let alone write it. It appeared that I had painted myself into a corner with my commercial success and as a result I felt a bit trapped. So, I prayed about it and put the intention out to the universe to help me find a way to make the personal, professional, and spiritual transformations in my life that I knew were crucial to my evolution and happiness.

Little by little everything started falling into place as I made the necessary changes in my life. There certainly were sacrifices involved, but I was willing to make them, and within a few years the things I had dreamt of started to become reality. *Gates of Gold*, the symphonic composition I had hoped to write, and knew was waiting out in the ether somewhere, finally materialized, as well as a whole new, supremely gratifying and meaningful life as a composer of concert music. The public's acceptance and appreciation of the music was thrilling beyond what I had imagined it might be, and I believe I know why, at least in part: I was living my truth and the music reflected that.

A more recent experience of this kind was the writing of this book. I first had the insight to write this book nine years ago. The title came first and I wrote one page and could go no further. I had finally gotten to a point in my life where I felt I had something important to share in words about creativity, but since I couldn't get past the first page, I had the feeling that perhaps I *still* had more to learn before a book could be written. Year after year I would take that one page out from time to time and try to develop it, but nothing would flow. However, *I knew* this book was out there waiting to be born. I just figured that it wasn't the right time yet. Finally in October of 2004 its time did come, and the book started unfolding effortlessly. The gestation period had reached maturation and the birthing process had commenced. Nature was once again doing what it does best: creating new life.

One might wonder though, if we are all creative, why is it so much more obvious in some than in others? Part of the problem stems from our early indoctrination in the misguided myth that says truly inspired creativity is only for a select, chosen few who have been "touched by the hand of God." The truth is, we are *all* touched by the hand of God. In fact, *we are the hand of God!* We are branches on the tree of Divine love and creativity. We are the fruits born *out of* the world, not *into* the world. As the philosopher Alan Watts put it in his lecture, *The Nature of Consciousness*, the world "peoples" just as an apple tree "apples."[13]

Why is it then that so many people seem blocked or "disconnected" from that endless flow of creativity and the source of creative energy? There are many possibilities. It could stem from our natural and intuitive creativity being suppressed or discouraged by parents or teachers when we were children, or from a mate, family members, or our peers in adulthood. Were there people in our lives that saw our creative potential and helped nurture it? Did we have access to "healthy" teachers who were intuitive and inspiring? Physicist David Bohm wrote in his book, *On Creativity*, "Generally speaking, what we learn as children, from parents, teachers, friends, and society in general, is to have a conformist, imitative, mechanical state of mind that does not present the disturbing danger of 'upsetting the applecart'."[14]

There are still other things to consider. Were the tools we needed to help us express our creativity available to us? Did we have access to an environment that was conducive to creativity, even if for part of the time? Any of these factors can certainly play a role in our creative development, and can influence the form and style of the creative expression we choose. However, despite any or all of the above reasons for not tapping into our creative truth, our creativity *must* be expressed and will continually seek a way to do so *no matter what*, because it is our nature to create. We *must* create. The need to create is so strong that when it is suppressed we run the risk of getting sick. To compensate we look for other avenues of excitement and stimulation to fill the void, but they prove to be temporary fixes that fall far short and create problems of their own. In reference to this, David Bohm continues, "So now we have seen that the artist, the musical composer, the architect, the scientist all feel a fundamental need to discover and create something new that is whole and total, harmonious and beautiful . . . it is probably what very large numbers of people in all walks of life are seeking when they attempt to escape the daily humdrum routine by engaging in every kind of entertainment, excitement, stimulation, change of occupation, and so forth, through which they ineffectively try to compensate for the unsatisfying narrowness and mechanicalness of their lives."[15]

Another issue that might present itself as a block to expressing our creativity is our attitude toward age. Some people might feel they are too old to bother exploring their creativity and might even think it silly, although I believe deep inside all of us we know this not to be true. However, some try to suppress that truth because to *really* look at it would then naturally incline us to take action, which might lead to ridicule, or having to bear hearing demeaning comments like, "Grow up!" or "Act your age!" or "Get a life!" Or we may be asked, "Are you getting senile?" or, "Is this your second childhood?" But what is so wrong with a person of *any* age wanting to learn how to paint, or dance, or play an instrument? *Nothing!* What is wrong with someone wanting to seek optimum health through expressing one's creative ideas and feelings? *Nothing!* Why must age have *any* bearing on whether we have "permission" to create or not? *It doesn't!* We must avoid falling victim to the mass social hypnosis concerning age. It is incorrect, counterproductive, and could be very destructive if taken to the extreme. Yes, our bodies age, but who we *really* are does not. The truth is we are eternal children who want to *play*, and this child-like creative spirit is our true nature and essence that must be allowed to live and express itself freely in order for us to be truly healthy in every way.

But doesn't creativity require craft? Ultimately no, but the more developed our craft is, the greater our freedom of expression. However, French artist Edouard Manet stated, "It is not enough to know your craft . . . you have to have feeling." Craft may be thought of as the "nuts and bolts" aspect of creative unfoldment that nearly anyone can learn. However, in the hands of someone truly creatively evolved, even craft itself can transform into its own expression of creative magic and become its own artform. A paintbrush is just a paintbrush, but in the hands of someone deeply in touch with their creative self, it becomes a magic wand. So, too, with a writer's pen, a conductor's baton, a flautist's flute, a person's "green thumb," and so on. I think of craft as the skill and technique we need, the vehicle that helps drive our inspiration, getting us where we want to go creatively. It is the language we use to communicate our ideas, however, *it is not the idea itself.* Using music composition as an example, Sufi mystic and musician Hazrat Inayat Khan wrote in his book, *The Mysticism of Sound and Music,* "It is not only the knowledge of technicality, of harmony, of theory that is sufficient; the composer needs tenderness of heart, open eyes to all beauty, the conception of what is beautiful, the true perception of sound and rhythm, and its expression in human nature."[16]

Though lacking craft does not mean we cannot communicate our creativity, the better our command of the language, and the more skillful we are with the tools and technique of our craft, the more fluidly and accurately we can get our creative intentions across. For example, as a composer, if I hear a certain sound "in my head," with a certain color and texture, how will I be able to materialize that without the experience derived from knowing the craft of orchestration well? If the craft of orchestrating music has become second nature to me, then I can effortlessly know how to mix the right tonal colors to achieve the desired results very spontaneously. It's very similar to how a painter mixes paint, or a chef mixes ingredients, adding a "pinch" of this or a "pinch" of that by "feel." This comes with experience and the best way to gain this experience is by just jumping in and trying. We can read books all we want, but theorizing about painting, for example, is obviously no match for mixing some paint together to create a desired color, and then brushing it on a canvas. Trial and error is one of several ways to become a skillful craftsman, trying new things and remembering the results. To a great degree, this is how I learned to do what I do best.

As for the difference between creativity and "art," what does it matter? Getting involved in such a subjective debate starts us venturing into the realm of the ego and I have little interest in going there. It's very dangerous territory that taints and discolors our creative truth and its fruits. It takes our focus away from what really matters most. *Creating* is the issue of importance, not labeling, judging, or posturing, which I find terribly distasteful. That's not to say that I don't have my own personal opinions, likes and dislikes, because I certainly do. But that does not give me the right or the authority to judge someone else's work as good or bad in a public forum, especially if the work has been done with love and the best of intentions. The same holds true for "mastery." In this lifetime do we ever really arrive at a point of ultimate mastery? And who determines where that point is? Who has been given that kind of authority to judge another person's creativity? Although we can get an intuitive sense of what mastery might be from what we feel inside, I believe our energy and attention can be much better directed to the cultivation of our creativity instead of wasting time intellectualizing about whether we are "masters" or not, or other such meaningless forays into the deluded world of the ego. It is better to focus on the *journey* toward mastery rather than being attached to the goal. It is important to intend what we want, but then we must ultimately let go of our attachment to the results, letting things unfold naturally through the power of our spirit, good intentions, and honest efforts. Once we have taken care of our part in this cosmic collaboration, it's best to let our Higher Power take care of orchestrating the rest.

It has become quite a challenge, though, to try to find our true selves in a world that is constantly sending out the wrong messages, misleading, manipulative messages that we must look a certain way to be loved, we must have such and such to be considered successful, must act our age, and live according to extremely biased religious and politically devised social edicts in order to be acceptable. The underlying message is, *conform*, be "good little soldiers." Many of us live in societies where individuality is actually discouraged and conformity is encouraged, whether overtly or covertly. So it's a battle from birth to be able to express our true selves because so few of us actually know who we really are. We are under a continual barrage of well-thought-out attempts to control our minds, even to the point of trying to control how we feel about ourselves. That is not only unacceptable, it is a violation of nature, *our* nature. How can somebody else tell us who we are or what we *should* be, and even imprison us in one way or another for not complying? We are even bullied concerning our beliefs in *God*, that if we don't toe the line and worship in a certain way, our worship will be considered unacceptable and therefore we will not only be cast out of the "Kingdom of God," worse still, we will burn in the fires of Hell for all eternity! That is absolute *insanity*. It's taken a lifetime of sincere, dedicated investigation and *unlearning* for me to free myself from the destructive guilt that this kind of brainwashing breeds. This mindless game of "spiritual one-upsmanship," where "we're saved and you're not," and "we're the chosen people and you're not," is so blatantly baseless, that I don't want to waste one more moment of my time addressing it anymore. And what is tragic is that many of us allow ourselves to actually *believe* it.

How can we even begin to express the uniqueness of our creative selves after such a blasphemous bombardment of mind-twisting, manipulative untruths? The absurdity of all this brings to mind a quote by Einstein, whose great wisdom and understanding are very fitting here: "Two things are infinite: the universe and human stupidity; and I'm not sure about the universe." I hope you can see why I brought this up. I have no agenda and nothing to sell when it comes to religion or anything else, so that was most certainly not the motivation. In fact, poet John Keats sums up my feelings about this issue very well: "Love is my religion." My point is that the bondage created by believing in this kind of negative, small-minded, ego-based one-upsmanship that has no basis in truth, most definitely can have a devastating effect not only on the natural unfolding of our creativity, but on all of creation. And how could it not? So, we must consider all of this when trying to figure out why we might be creatively blocked. We read in the Gospel of John, "Know the truth and the truth will set you free."[17] Once we know the truth, *our* truth, then we can be free to create. And once we're free, there is no safety to be found in turning back.

On our path of creative self-discovery, it is not necessary to limit ourselves to one form of creative expression. Although I am a composer of music, along the way I also became a photographer, a poet, an artist, and now an author. I began writing poetry in my early twenties because I needed to express myself in words as well as music. I needed to "talk" to someone in a more conventional way, and that someone was, first of all, myself. It turns out that poetry was a natural extension of music anyway, with its rhythmic and melodic flow. So although I was traveling somewhat new territory, it was also territory that was familiar to me in some ways.

There was a time when I would sit to write poetry and allow myself to write anything that came into my mind, *without judgment*. I wanted the raw data, the unfiltered feelings, emotions, and thoughts to flow through without my intellect getting in the way and masking the truth, with all its accrued negative baggage, prejudices, and judgments born out of social, religious, and cultural indoctrination. I would do the same thing years later when I composed "Forgiveness," from the composition *Awakening*. I just sat at the piano and played whatever came to me, and recorded it. I played for around 7 minutes and later listened to it. Then, I just cleaned it up, softened the rough edges and orchestrated it. I did not want my intellect to get in the way. I was trying to find the real me, the real message, and not the one I thought others would like or expected to hear. Thinking is the enemy of creativity. I wanted to *feel*, to listen to my soul, not my mind. And by staying out of the way, not imposing myself on the music, the music taught me a great lesson. I later learned that the composition *Forgiveness* was presented to me as a model from which to learn *how* to forgive when I was finding it nearly impossible to forgive someone for hurting me so deeply. My staying out of the way allowed this to happen. It was so interesting that recently I came across a quote by author George Kneller, from his book *The Art and Science of Creativity*, that stated what I had already experienced: "At some stage in the process of creation, the creative product—whether painting, poem, or scientific theory— takes on a life of its own and transmits its own needs to its creator. It stands apart from him and summons material from his subconscious. The creator, then, must know when to cease directing his work and when to allow it to direct him. He must know, in short, when his work is likely to be wiser than he."[18] I have found this to be true of all the compositions I have written since the onset of what I consider my spiritual awakening, beginning in 1993. I'm *still* learning from those compositions, *still* discovering many valuable life lessons through them: compassion, forgiveness, joy; peace, tranquility, and the beauty of silence; the unity in diversity, why I am here, and above all, *love*. I don't think I would be learning these things from the music if I had let my intellect get in the way. It required letting go of all of that. Detaching from the mind.

There are times when I become too saturated by conventional music and need to step away from it for a while in order to become re-energized and infused with new life. Yet, I need to express myself in some artistic ways in order to stay creatively, physically, and emotionally healthy. But that took some time for me to learn. I remember early on during my time at Columbia Pictures, I happily worked from morning until night, seven days a week, writing and writing and writing, both alone and with as many people who would collaborate with me. Being under the umbrella of the Columbia Pictures name, there was never a lack of wonderful writers to work with. I was one happy workaholic. But one day, the friend who signed me to Columbia Pictures as their first staff songwriter, said something to me that made me stop and think. He said, "How can you write about life if you don't live one?" He encouraged me to balance my life out and take some time off each week and enjoy life in some other ways: take a drive up the California coast, go hiking, spend some time by the sea. That was some of the most valuable advice I have ever been given, and it has never left me. I can't imagine living any other way now and can see more clearly that stepping back from time to time actually helps us to become *more* creative and *more* productive, adding more depth and color to our creative expression. But although I find it necessary to step away from music from time to time, the creative drive still remains strong in me, as does the need to express myself creatively in some fulfilling way. So I allow myself to explore other aspects of my creative self during those respites from music. That's where photography and poetry, art and writing have filled that need perfectly, and I believe that there are other wonderful and exciting expressions of creativity that I have yet to discover in myself.

Photography came along much later in my life. It really kicked into high gear after the near-death experience I had in Singapore in 1994.

In early 1995 when I was back in Southern California healing, photography became the best medicine on my road to recovery. Perhaps it was a deeply instinctive thing, but in order to heal, I needed to withdraw to the quiet of nature, to ride the waves of its ocean, to align myself with its melodic flow, and to entrain with its rhythm. Photography led me there. Looking through the viewfinder, I was able to discover the unspeakable beauty of worlds within the world that I never knew existed because I had never taken the time to notice. I was finally taking the time to really open my heart and quiet my mind in order to see so much more of the Divine creativity everywhere that had previously escaped me because of my lack of attention. Photography taught me how to paint with light, to compose music with light. Trying different combinations of film, filters, and lenses, natural light itself became a fascinating study in sound and vibration, and how its different qualities influenced the mood and subtle orchestration of the photographic compositions. The soft early morning light and the golden light of the late afternoon and early evening became the designated concert time when the atmosphere came alive with the sound of illumined music. And most interesting of all on this journey was that the experience gave me a better chance to see the beauty of my own soul in the photographs. They have a distinct and unique personality; *my* personality as reflected in the tree that I am, and the flower that I am, and the sky that I am.

Sometimes I need to express myself in different artistic ways in order to stay creatively, physically, and emotionally healthy. The fruits of our diverse talents make life so colorful and full and we should not be afraid to express the different shades and hues of who we are. Previously, I had been much too busy "spinning my wheels" in pursuit of things that were noble, but of much less importance, to actually notice so much of the Divine beauty all around me that I had been missing. In this way, getting sick was a wakeup call that offered me the opportunity to slow down and look all around me with new eyes, to listen with new ears to all the beauty I had never tuned into, and to feel with a new heart. I needed to learn the greater lessons of life that would help me to evolve to a higher level of awareness, to a better way of living, and a deeper way of loving. I needed to learn a different kind of music, the music that was hidden in the unexplored depths of my soul, to compose with shadow and light as well as with the dots of intention and potentiality written on musical manuscript, choosing from the vast palette of nature before me and all around me, to create a body of work that would paint the beauty of the world as seen through my eyes.

When a creator of beauty brings forth a work that says so simply what every book in a library combined could never begin to express, then he or she has found home: the house of belonging. It could be in the stroke of an artist's brush or a composer's melody. It may be painted in a poet's perfect metaphor, or in a dance company's magical moment of moving as one body. It could be in the joy we feel from the euphoria others experience when tasting something we cooked that was infused with all our love and caring. It is also the soft music in the loving words of a tender heart . . . The form of our creativity is not as important as the loving essence within a given form, because that love is the foundation of our creative expression itself, eternal and indestructible.

I truly believe we are all Divinely creative. We just need to realize and graciously accept it, and then access it by listening to our soul. We can accomplish this by allowing ourselves to feel with our hearts and see through our eye of enlightenment. Perhaps it is through our unbending need to create, and the fortitude, resilience, and power that is born out of that fearless, courageous pursuit to be who we *really* are, that a ripple effect is created throughout the infinite ocean of things and ideas, causing a creative, magnetic wave that synchronistically orchestrates the perfect placement of all the pieces of the grand puzzle. This is the preamble that choreographs the cosmic ballet that brings our creative wishes to fruition. We are all capable, to one degree or another, of materializing the creative wishes of our hearts, relative to our experience, circumstances, and where we are on our designated paths. But we have to *believe* we can. We must *allow* creation to flow freely and not resist it, judge it, or question it, secure in knowing that we are worthy of the creative bounty that the universe has to offer. We must allow it to just *be*, to unfold naturally and spontaneously and to know it as truth. We must experience our Higher Power through our creative expression, through the love we materialize in a spectrum of creative ways. Then we can truly grasp the depth of our infinite creative potential and feel free to express it without fear of judgment, *knowing* it is an expression of God, of love, of the Cosmic Mind. Then we open ourselves up to the world of all creative possibilities through the universal insight we call "imagination."

"Highly creative people, like saints, testify to the dazzling multi-dimensions and holy contradictions of life. Disregarding personal happiness, they come into the world as messengers of the unfolding truth, motivated by a cosmic imperative. Because they are brave, all humankind becomes a bit braver; because they struggle to achieve fulfillment, the integrity of the species is enhanced. Their vision, so disturbingly acute, permits everyone to see more clearly a reality that is always present but, for most of us, obscured by ego-induced myopia."[19]

Marilyn Whiteside
American author

Creativity Quotations

Creativity Quotations

"God didn't have time to make a nobody, only a somebody.
I believe that each of us has God-given talents within us
waiting to be brought to fruition."

Mary Kay Ash
American businesswoman

"There are two ways of being creative. One can sing and
dance. Or one can create an environment in which singers
and dancers flourish."

Warren G. Bennis
American psychologist

"Make visible what, without you, might perhaps never have
been seen."

Robert Bresson
French filmmaker

"If I create from the heart, nearly everything works; if from the head, almost nothing."

Marc Chagall
Russian-born French artist

"The most beautiful thing we can experience is the mysterious. It is the source of all true art and science."

Albert Einstein
German-born American physicist

"We have all been granted the power of creation by God. If we use this power to the maximum, we will be able to change the world in but a moment."[20]

Masaru Emoto
Japanese author and doctor of alternative medicine

"Genuinely creative work is, at core, a form of worship, an excursion into the unconscious—'the house of God'—in an effort to manifest the source of life through ideas and products, as holy people reveal it through the quality of their lives . . . Those who create must be willing and able to tear down existing ideas and structures (and even their own personalities) to make way for the new and untried. They must abandon tradition, with its certainties, in favor of innovation, with its uncertainties."

Marilyn Whiteside
American author

Creativity and Imagination

Chapter Two
Creativity and Imagination

"Imagination is the beginning of creation.
You imagine what you desire; you will what you imagine;
and at last you create what you will."

George Bernard Shaw
Irish dramatist, literary critic, Nobel Prize winner

Every day we imagine many things. To imagine is to create at a very fundamental level. What we have become and what we have created in our lives is very much a product of our imagination. The Buddha, Siddhartha Gautama, stated, "All that we are is a result of what we have thought." *We are* our imagination and part of a greater, cosmic imagination. We *are* the universe creating, and those open enough to that creative cosmic energy become channels for its beauty, love and creativity. We "feel" it and have a greater sense of being tapped into something much more than we appear to be. Those who have not yet experienced this kind of cosmic connectedness are still creating all the time, but their awareness of it, and the full force of their creative potential, is often hindered by the illusory nature of their five-sense experience. There is much more beyond what we can see, touch, taste, hear, and smell, and a wealth of credible examples exists to substantiate this. Let's explore for a moment the potential influence of past lives on creativity.

Perhaps some are freer to create than others because they are more in tune with the universal library of knowledge that they have brought with them to this life. For example, there are many children who seem beyond their years and have a kind of wisdom that defies their age and experience, old souls that draw from the experiences of many lifetimes to fuel their imagination. "Consider, for example, Wolfgang Amadeus Mozart, the world-famous eighteenth-century composer. At the age of four he wrote a piano concerto, a sonata, and several minuets. His compositions were anything but simple, but were nevertheless technically accurate. Think about that for a moment . . . four years old! By the age of seven he had composed a full-length opera . . . How does one explain Mozart's genius, particularly at such an early age? Reincarnation might suggest Mozart in a previous life was a musician and composer. This type of reasoning would say that Mozart had already accomplished much of the necessary groundwork for his skills and his genius and when he was born Wolfgang Amadeus Mozart, he was well primed to begin work at a very early age."[21] Another article, *Transmigration of the Soul*, states under the heading "Artistic Genius:" "Some of the musical greats of the last few centuries leave us wondering about reincarnation. Mozart was composing entire symphonies by the time he was six years old. Beethoven and Bach were similar. Genius in almost every art form has emerged at almost unbelievable ages showing a proclivity for talent far beyond any mortal logic."[22]

Whether you resonate in part or in whole with this idea, the past life factor in one's creative evolution is, at minimum, something very interesting to ponder, but also something to be seriously considered in light of a growing amount of credible information. I was fortunate enough to have been invited to a special screening of the movie *A Brief History of Time* at Caltech in the early '90s, in which physicist Stephen Hawking himself attended and spoke. The small auditorium was filled with some of the greatest minds on the planet, including many of the physicists who were actually interviewed in the movie.

The power of the collective intelligence and creative energy in that room was unfathomable, yet something Stephen Hawking said suddenly gave me my first real sense of understanding what reincarnation might be. Everything I had heard or read before on the subject never seemed to make much sense to me. But what Stephen Hawking said, most certainly created an epiphany: "If an astronaut falls into a black hole, its mass will increase. Eventually the energy equivalent of that extra mass will be returned to the universe in the form of radiation. Thus, in a sense, the astronaut will be recycled . . . The only feature of the astronaut that will survive would be his mass or energy."[23] I immediately thought, *Oh, this must be reincarnation!* It was such a simple, non-threatening way of explaining the subject, although I don't think that was necessarily his intent. Anyway, this is what I understood from it and its significance has only increased over the years. Everything in the physical universe is indestructible energy, floating in what has been called, "energy soup."[24] And according to Deepak Chopra, "today's science acknowledges the inseparability of information fields, energy fields, and matter fields."[25] So then, if energy and information are inseparable, it would stand to reason that the knowledge contained within the astronaut's energy that Stephen Hawking spoke of, would not be lost. It would just be recycled back into the universe as someone like Mozart, or me, or you, for example.

In researching reincarnation further, I was surprised by the number of noted people of the past who clearly embraced this belief, including: Benjamin Franklin, Jack London, Mark Twain, Leo Tolstoy, Henry Ford, Walt Whitman, General George Patton, William Wordsworth, Socrates, Ralph Waldo Emerson, Henry David Thoreau, and the list goes on![26] Even Jesus brings it to light in Matthew 17:12-13, when he speaks about John the Baptist not being recognized as the reincarnation of Elijah.[27] We must keep in mind that although this concept has been comparatively foreign to Westerners, it has been considered common knowledge by a very large cross-section of the world population and has been for thousands of years, most notably Hindus and Buddhists.

Coming from a Christian upbringing, entertaining the idea of past lives and reincarnation was strictly frowned upon. As a result, I steered clear of it most of my life for fear of being "damned." Looking back I can see very clearly now how fear and false information were ritually used to keep people from considering anything beyond the dogma of Judeo-Christian doctrines, keeping us shackled in the politically motivated mental prison of so many organized religions. But as my own experiences with the mystical continued to unfold all over the world, not even the bondage of Western religion could keep me from examining everything, questioning everything in search of the truth. And as a result of my increasing exposure to a wealth of new experiences, especially from years of traveling through, and living in Asia, I could no longer ignore or deny the strong probability of other realities and other truths, including reincarnation. However, these new experiences were not limited to Asia; they existed everywhere. This knowledge is part of the universal fabric, and becoming awakened to it has allowed me to live and express my innate creativity more freely and with a greater understanding of its nature. I am not trying to sell anyone on the idea of reincarnation. It is presented as one of many possibilities in the quest to both understand and explain some very magical and otherwise unexplainable aspects of creative unfoldment, including many creators' seeming ability to see beyond the present reality. One of the most intuitive and eloquent writers on the subject of creativity is Marilyn Whiteside, who so insightfully wrote in her article, "Rare Beasts in the Sheepfold," in *The Journal of Creative Behavior.* "Less shackled by the common illusions of time, space and personality, some creators are mystics and seers. They reach into antiquity and bring the past into the present; they explore the future and return as harbingers of events yet to come."[28]

We can see from the artifacts left by our ancient ancestors that there has always been a need in us to create. They created early versions of things we still use today to express our creativity. They carved flutes out of wood. They made drums from wood and animal hides.

They painted on cave walls and rocks. They fashioned tools from the raw materials available to them, including *iron meteorites*. They made cosmetics and jewelry with which to adorn themselves and enhance their beauty, making do with whatever resources and materials they had available. The same is true today, in that no matter what our circumstances, we can still use our imagination to create new things that are reflective of our own unique spirits from those same resources and materials that our ancestors used thousands or more years ago.

I am always so amazed at the depth of so many people's creative brilliance. The fact that people can create beautiful, clever, and oftentimes very useful things out of seemingly nothing, makes me shake my head in awe. Once I see what has been created from just *a thought*, it makes so much sense to me and I think to myself, *Why didn't I think of that?* I feel sure many of us say that very same thing. People find rocks and wood on the beach and create beauty with them. They find dead wood in a forest and make jewelry boxes and furniture out of it. What about the "Hula Hoop" (it's a plastic tube!), "Slinky" (a metal coil!), "Slip and Slide" (a sheet of vinyl!). How about "Pet Rocks" and "Wacky Wallwalkers???" Born out of a conversation among a few friends discussing how nice it would be to have a no-maintenance pet, a million Pet Rocks were sold in a few months! An article from *The Encyclopedia of Pop Culture* stated, concerning these products that were basically something made out of "nothing:" "It gave people a few moments of absolutely meaningless pleasure in a troubled world—no small accomplishment." Ken Hakuta, who brought Wacky Wallwalkers to the world, observed, "If there were more fads there would probably be a lot fewer psychiatrists. . . . Instead of paying $100-an-hour therapy sessions, you could just get yourself a couple of Wacky Wallwalkers (a rubber toy that sticks and wiggles on a wall, which earned Hakuta $20 million) and a Slinky and lock yourself up in a room for a couple of hours. When you came out, you'd be fine."[29] It may oversimplify a cure for the mass neurosis of our society, but it is also very true that even such simple and seemingly silly creations have great value and do a great service to us. In this case, they make us laugh. It's good for our health. If we have good health, we have the energy to be creative. And these examples can serve as an inspiration to us that the power of an idea, even the simplest idea, with the proper follow-through and intentions, can create great prosperity and happiness for both the creator and for the recipients of that creative expression.

There are untapped goldmines all around us just waiting to be discovered just as the above examples illustrate, and basically all it takes to access this wealth is to tap into the greatest goldmine of all: our imagination. All it takes is the spark of an idea to set our creative fires ablaze. And the good news is, we all have that creative fire within us. All of us possess our own unique creative talent and beauty and we would do well to be true to those gifts. For one it is music, for another it is sewing, for yet another it is woodworking. For others it is exploring sub-atomic particles in search of meaning, or a scientist's search to better understand the mechanisms and origin of disease. And then there are those who have been able to develop more than one of the many varieties of creative expression simultaneously.

We are our greatest creative resource. We don't need to be graduates of conservatories to create or perform beautiful music. We don't even need an instrument to create music, for that matter. Once again we can look deep within ourselves and be the instruments of God. Physically, we are the instruments of our Higher Power. Spiritually, *we are that Higher Power.* We can sing the songs of our soul and create rhythm with our hands or with things that we find around us. We can draw and we can literally create beautiful art out of what most might consider "junk." We can write poetry and stories and recite them, sparking the imagination of listeners by being storytellers, just as many ancient cultures, such as the Native Americans have done. That requires no materials *at all.* If the will to create is strong enough, *and it is*, nothing can stop us from creating. The only thing that can *really* stop us is *us.*

It should be reassuring to everyone that no matter how our achievements are compared to the achievements of others, no one else can do what we are here to do. Each of us is here to bring forth what only *we* can bring forth and therefore we should not judge our accomplishments by what society dictates as having great value or not. Societies' fear-based mandates and opinions are not an accurate or fair measuring stick for assessing the value of our work, nor the basis for establishing our self-worth. We must be true to ourselves and not spend our lives imitating others in a fearful "sheep-going-to-the-slaughter" procession, confirming German philosopher Arthur Schopenhauer's words, "We forfeit three-fourths of ourselves in order to be like other people." Imitation is a means to an end, an important part of our learning process. But at a very pivotal point on our path of creative self-discovery, it becomes crucial not only to our survival, but to our truly *living* a healthy, fulfilling life, to make the *choice* to fearlessly be who we *really* are and to fulfill what we came here to do. Psychologist Rollo May, in his book, *The Courage to Create*, believes that, "If you do not express your original ideas, if you do not listen to your own being, you will have betrayed yourself,"[30] and that, according to Indian spiritual teacher Sai Baba, would be a tragedy.

Whatever ideas one can imagine, are the seeds, the potentiality for their fulfillment. *Whatever* we can imagine is something that not only has the potential of being materialized, but perhaps has already been materialized somewhere, past, present, future, or running simultaneously in a parallel reality. According to an article in *Astronomy Magazine*, "If time travel is—even only in theory—possible, this then means that all times (past, present & future) of this Universe must exist simultaneously."[31] Although I don't have a mathematical equation to prove this or the scientific language to better articulate it, I do have an intuitive sense of its being true. Zen scholar D.T. Suzuki states, "In this spiritual world there are no time divisions such as the past, present, and future; for they contracted themselves into a single moment of the present . . ." When people say, "The past is the past," I always seem to intuitively balk. Although a particular incident might appear unchangeable due to past actions, its repercussions live on in the present and into the future. So, too, concerning the fruits of our imagination.

"Imagination is more important than knowledge.
Knowledge is limited. Imagination encircles the world."

Albert Einstein
German-born American physicist

Imagination Quotations

Imagination Quotations

"What is now proved was once only imagined."

William Blake
English mystic, poet, painter, and engraver

"All riches have their origin in mind. Wealth is in ideas—not money."

Robert Collier
American motivational author

"You'll see it when you believe it."

Dr. Wayne Dyer
Psychologist, author, and self-help speaker

"Logics will get you from A to B, imagination will take you everywhere."

Albert Einstein
German-born American physicist

"What we imagine in our minds becomes our world."[32]

Masaru Emoto
Japanese author and doctor of alternative medicine

"Man's mind once stretched by a new idea, never regains its original dimension."

Oliver Wendell Holmes
American poet, essayist, and physician

"I saw the angel in the marble and carved until I set him free."

Michelangelo
Italian artist, sculptor, and painter

"The world is but a canvas to the imagination."

Henry David Thoreau
American philosopher and naturalist

"The poorest man is not without a cent, but without a dream."

Unknown Author

"If you can imagine it, you can achieve it; if you can dream it, you can become it."

William Arthur Ward
Author and American college administrator

Creativity and Education

Chapter Three
Creativity and Education

"I have never let my schooling interfere with my education."
Mark Twain
American humorist, author, and wit

When I have the opportunity to walk into a classroom or lecture hall as a guest speaker, I sometimes say to the students, "OK, what are you going to teach me today?" The same kind of thought also comes to mind when I stand on a podium to conduct an orchestra or walk outside to face the world. Despite the outward appearance of sameness or familiarity, every moment is different and every situation offers a unique opportunity to learn something new. In fact, the more I learn the more I realize how much more there is still left to learn. It's infinite! So far in this lifetime, though, it feels like I have only been able to access a tiny bit of knowledge compared to what there is to know. But as long as I know what's most important, then that's at least a good foundation from which to build.

"Without going outside, you may know the whole world!"

Lao Tzu

Concerning industrialized society's idea of "educated" and "uneducated" people, I have met those with no formal education who seem to have the wisdom of the Universe and the intuitive knowledge of the ages. Many have never left the perimeter of their own yard, yet they have a knowingness of the world that defies their circumstances. It became second nature for me to walk into a little shop in Kathmandu Nepal, for example, and look into the eyes of a clerk, and *know* that this person was no stranger to me. And it was so interesting that months later when I met her father, who is a shepherd from a remote village halfway between Kathmandu and Mt. Everest, and I told him what I had experienced, he said in Nepali, "Doesn't everybody know that?" How *great* it was to be speaking the same "language." What took *me*, a well educated, well traveled, cultured, "civilized" man from the richest country in the world, more than 40 years to come to know was second nature to an "uneducated" shepherd from the second poorest country in the world.

I have heard more than one modern philosopher state that we are not really learning anything, we are just *remembering*, remembering what we already know; accessing the infinite intelligence, wisdom, and knowledge that are found in every cell of our being. The Polish-born novelist Joseph Conrad said, "The mind of man is capable of anything because everything is in it, all the past as well as the future." But when "maya," the illusions of our world causes us to forget who we are and what we know, a poet wrote, "sometimes it is necessary to reteach a thing its loveliness . . . until it flowers again from within."[33]

Unfortunately, so much of what we are taught and grow up believing has no basis in truth. We need to fashion lives based on accurate knowledge, but few are those who have the courage to question the authority of what we have been taught and, at minimum, take the personal responsibility to do something about it where needed. Why is this? Perhaps because the responsibilities that go along with having to unlearn falsehoods often require making changes in our thinking and belief systems, which may in turn require making changes to the foundation of how we live our lives. "Old beliefs die hard even when demonstrably false."[34] Therefore, many people prefer not to accept those responsibilities, not wanting to upset the status quo in their life, often hiding behind the false notion that "ignorance is bliss." Ignorance may *seem* to be bliss, but only for a while. Soon enough the truth starts staring us in the face and relentlessly calling out in quiet moments. That's probably why many people try to keep *really* busy, distracting and numbing themselves with any number of comparatively unimportant things, blocking out their inner voice so they don't have to listen to the infinite intelligence of their soul speaking. But in order to get to the core essence of our creative selves, we often have to *unlearn* many of the things that we have been indoctrinated with since birth. We *do not* belong in a state of ignorance. We belong in the light, the light that contains energy and information. *Accurate* information. *The truth*. Don't be afraid to "stir the soup" or be the "salt in the stew" in the pursuit of living a creatively truthful life.

There are many different ways to learn, depending on our personality, circumstances, and individual needs, but all must ultimately be based in truth. Apache artist Allen Houser offers his own thoughts on this: "One way of learning art is to choose a master and then to try to copy that master; another way is to take off on your own and then try to master whoever you are." Most of what I learned about composing music and all the magic that goes with it, I *did not* learn in school. In fact, although I have a degree in music education, I am basically self-taught in composition, orchestration, and conducting. I learned more from keen observation, humbly asking questions, and trusting my intuition, than *anything* I ever learned either in music school or from private teachers. I even learn a lot from the people and things I *don't* appreciate as well as from the people and things I do. In this regard I have an experiential understanding of author Arthur Koestler's words: "Creative activity could be described as a type of learning process where teacher and pupil are located in the same individual."

But having a wonderful and inspiring mentor, or being able to attend famous schools may be the perfect thing for someone else. It just wasn't the way things unfolded for me, and looking at the overview of my life and life's work, I'm grateful for that. I believe that if I had been too closely influenced by any one person or ideology, it could have been very detrimental to the blossoming of my individuality. English author Beatrix Potter seemed to have shared the same sentiment: "Thank goodness I was never sent to school; it would have rubbed off some of the originality."

Concerning those whose creative path is best explored, at least in part, with a mentor, the relationship between a student and teacher is like a marriage, or the interaction between a parent and child, or even a doctor and patient, depending on the level of maturity. The foundation of the relationship must be built upon *trust*. Studying privately with a mentor can be a very emotionally intimate experience in which we must allow ourselves to be vulnerable, because especially in the arts, we are striving to express our deepest feelings and emotions through the medium of creativity that feels most comfortable and natural to us. A mentor is supposed to help us gain the means to be able to express our souls freely and effortlessly, and that usually requires digging deep. A really *great* teacher will be able to help us to do this in an honorable and caring way without imposing their personal or artistic agenda, being more of an inspiring guide than an egotistical, dictatorial bully, someone who can help bring out and develop a student's individuality rather than squash it with dogmatic opinions. To quote Galileo, "You cannot teach a man anything. You can only help him find it within himself." I believe that such inspired teachers are the exception and not the rule, so it becomes a situation of "buyer beware!" for students trying to find the right teacher. As usual, trust your gut and never be afraid to question authority.

At this point in my life, where I am now acknowledged as an American composer of note (no pun intended), I find it kind of amusing when people ask me, so excitedly and with such great anticipation,

"Who did you study with?" or "Where did you go to school?" like *those* are the be-all, end-all secrets to what they perceive as my success. Because the music I am associated with, and the nature of my life's work are gratefully held in high esteem, many people seem to buy into the fantasy that perhaps I graduated from a famous conservatory and was the star pupil of some trendy, iconic, idiosyncratic composer who wears a cape and beret and smokes a cigarette from a long cigarette holder, someone with a clichéd foreign accent and says things like, "Well my dear . . . Oh yes, quite, quite . . ." (I find it rather odd how some non-British in the arts have mysteriously acquired a British accent . . .) This kind of prefab, stereotypical Hollywood-type delusion is a symptom of the general mass social hypnosis, a twisted myth that is greatly a product perpetuated by the media, and the empty pretensions of our culture. The same goes for the fallacy that a person has to be miserable, down and out, and some kind of borderline lunatic in order to create deep and meaningful works of art. Yes, many highly creative people seem "odd" compared to those in the mainstream, but society often over-romanticizes this, making too many allowances and excuses for the abhorrent behavior of some in the arts, passing it off as the byproduct of "genius." It's nonsense. Complete trash. "Genius" has no partnership with immorality. In fact I believe true genius is the summit of morality.

People generally seem quite surprised when I tell them that I'm self-taught. A kind of stunned silence fills the atmosphere, I guess because I don't fit the stereotype (thank God!). But my being self-taught is the truth and I have no fear in telling it. No one can argue with a person's success, especially when it is achieved with honor and integrity. The quality and success of a person's work is its own testimony that requires no trumpeting on his or her part. I do not hesitate telling students in a half-joking way that basically, my "classical" training was watching Bugs Bunny cartoons when they ask about my early studies in music. It's a bit of an exaggeration of course, but I did learn from *listening* . . . listening to just about everything that came within earshot of my path, from rock and roll to R&B to jazz to gospel to the amazing underscores of cartoons that often contained a wealth of the classical repertoire. And many of the Hollywood film composers were "serious" composers who came from the great Western European tradition. Some, like Erich Wolfgang Korngold, whose musical scores include *Robinhood* and *Kings Row*, among many others, did not aspire to work in Hollywood. But due to the horrors happening in his homeland during the Second World War, Hollywood provided a new and safe home for him and his family, as well as employment. Even the television music of the 1960's was so inventive and more often than not was written by very skilled and inspired composers who just chose to make their living in that burgeoning medium at the time. It didn't matter how the music was labeled, or who wrote it. If it was good it was *good* and I liked it.

Music is music to me and I don't like to get into labeling and compartmentalizing it as "black" music or "white" music, "classical" or "pop" . . . Why should I be so concerned with *that?* I have no interest in such a waste of my time and attention because it is just one more ugly expression of the fragmentation that tears our societies and world apart. It is a reflection of a much larger issue in our social consciousness that is destructive and causes alienation instead of integration. It is yet another blaring example of the lack of insight into the true nature and underlying oneness of all things. The wisdom of Indian spiritual teacher Paramahansa Yogananda, author of the beautifully written book, *Autobiography of a Yogi*, teaches us that, "Divisions are imaginary lines drawn by small minds." But we can choose to see beyond the veil of such socially divisive untruths.

If the music I listened to as a child touched my soul in some beautiful way, I loved it and learned from it. All of it was extremely valuable and somehow all of it is a part of who I have become, as has the music that channels through me; the music that makes people happy and feel inspired. I made the best with what I had access to and I feel my diverse background is *very* rich as a result. And being intimately familiar with all the various styles of music certainly was a huge advantage when I began working in Hollywood. There is a premium paid for that kind of diverse knowledge, especially if it can be accessed quickly and accurately.

My parents did not have the money to send me to a prestigious conservatory or university. I never had the opportunity to go to one of those fancy summer music camps for the privileged few who had money. In fact, my summer camp was unfortunately an inner city *Boys Club* where most of a child's time was spent struggling for survival. There were no lakes, no fields, and no forest. There was no canoeing and singing around the campfire. This was concrete jungle stuff, sitting on a hard floor. I was probably the only kid who wished the summer would end so school could start! Going back to school was a welcomed *reprieve* from just trying to stay alive all summer. My point is that although those fancy privileged opportunities can be really wonderful for the fortunate few who can afford them, they are no guarantee of success. And likewise, the lack of those opportunities will not prevent a person with great spirit and passion from succeeding either. This I know to be true. It's not about external things. It's all about what we do with what we have, and the quality of *who and what we are*. Our *spirit*. That's what *really* matters. I share this so that those who believe they have limited resources and opportunities, will hopefully be encouraged that no matter what their circumstances are, nothing can stop them from living their creative truth if they want it badly enough. The same philosophy applies to just about everything in life. And for those who *do* have the golden opportunities to study with famous teachers, attend famous universities, and have enlightening experiences at music camps and festivals, I say *"go for it!"* and get the most out of the privilege. There's no need to apologize for your good fortune. Just be sure you make the best of the opportunity.

The school of life is in session every moment of every day. It is not limited to the noble halls of a famous university. In fact, with few wonderful exceptions, I don't believe that *real* knowledge, practical knowledge, is found through institutionalized education, especially in the arts. Author Helen Keller stated something similar: "College isn't the place to go for ideas." I remember befriending two composers at the famous MacDowell Colony, the artist colony where we were all given fellowships. Once we got to know one another other better, they confessed they were very "suspicious" of me when I first arrived because I worked in *Hollywood* as well as in the concert world. So I found it very ironic that the first question they asked me was, "Tell us how to make money in music!" One had a masters degree in composition and the other a doctorate in the same, from one of the oldest and most prestigious university music schools in America. And although they particularly enjoyed studying with a key teacher at that university, they were very bitter that one very important aspect of their education was not addressed. Their education *did not* provide them with the practical knowledge and skills that could help them to apply that highbrow education *to the real world*. It didn't teach them *how to make a living*. Talent is only the ticket into the ballpark. In order to get out onto the playing field you must also be very resourceful, flexible, and versatile, and have developed good "people skills" to help turn that talent into something tangible. In order to have good people skills, you usually need to be a fairly well-balanced human being with decent values and good intuition. You must be honest, equitable, and ethical. I don't recall any courses in school geared toward this end.

I couldn't wait to get out in the professional world and live my dreams. Looking back, I can honestly say that university was much more difficult than the real working professional world turned out to be, because in the real world your true value is not based on your grades or talent alone. The quality of person you are and how easy you are to get along with is as important as your talent and technical ability. Institutes of higher education place too much emphasis on technical dazzlement, and it is brought to light in the book *The Transformative Vision* that "Virtuosity has little to do with true creativity."[35] In this regard, institutional education too often seems like some kind of testosterone decathlon. You know: *higher, faster, louder!* This brought to mind something I read recently by physicist Fritjof Capra, author of *The Tao of Physics*, in a conversation with *New Dimensions Radio's* Michael Toms, that may give some insight into the root of this mindset: "We have overemphasized self-assertion and have neglected integration. We have favored competition and neglected cooperation; we have favored analysis and neglected synthesis; have emphasized expansion and exploitation and have neglected conservation, and so on. These values that the Chinese call yang, that are the favorite ones in our society, are also the values of patriarchal culture. The feminist movement points out that the Cartesian worldview and this yang-oriented value system have been supported by the patriarchy. But like the Cartesian worldview, patriarchy is now in its decline. It's a slow and painful decline but it is definitely progressing, and we are gradually seeing the feminist perspective becoming an essential part of the new vision of reality."[36]

Indian mystic J. Krishnamurti said, "The function of education is to help you from childhood not to imitate anybody, but be yourself all the time." However, very often in school, as long as you regurgitate the slop you are force fed, without any rebuttal, you get your piece of cheese at the end of the maze. But what good is *that?* You have to pay tens of thousands of dollars to get a pat on the head for being a good little soldier? Is *that* education? Not in my opinion. Einstein said, "It is, in fact, nothing short of a miracle that the modern methods of instruction have not entirely strangled the holy curiosity of inquiry." The knowledge doled out in educational institutions is generally very slanted and biased because there are often any number of agendas behind it, a truthful education not generally being one of them. A lot of the information is absolutely *false.* What's passed off as history, in particular, is a complete joke, a sham, and blatant political propaganda! People are paying huge sums of money to be very often indoctrinated with *lies,* and are rewarded with a diploma for parroting back those same lies. This is not my idea of a real education. This is not my idea of a good investment. And this is certainly not an expression of creativity *at all.* In fact, it is the antithesis of creativity.

I am a big believer in "learn as you go," and an Estonian proverb states very similarly, "The work will teach you how to do it." I learned more about music and the music business from just being in the professional environment I wished to be a part of, around the people who were already doing what I hoped to do, keeping my eyes and ears wide open to everything around me. I was like a *sponge* soaking it all in. I remember, for years I wished that I never had to go to sleep because there were so many exciting things to learn and so much I wanted to do with all the new things I was learning every day. Time seemed to go by so quickly. This is a far cry from being bored to tears in a classroom listening to instructors who acted as if teaching was the last thing in the world they wished they were doing, teaching from a syllabus that they might not have actually believed in or approved of themselves. Let's face it, a great teacher, like *anything* of great value, is hard to find and worth *a lot*. Fortunately I had a few, but one teacher in particular, made all the other torturous time I spent in four years of university worth it. Twenty-five years later, when I told him this, he said, "I didn't teach you anything," and my reply was, "Maybe so, but I learned a lot from you."

"The Wu Li Master dances with his student. The Wu Li Mater does not teach, but the student learns." This is from the beautifully written book, *The Dancing Wu Li Masters (An Overview of the New Physics)* by Gary Zukav.[37] ("Wu Li" is the Chinese word for physics. Its poetic meaning is: "Pattern of organic energy.") The teacher I mentioned didn't seem to really fit the mold of the typical institutional academician, and although his teaching style seemed comparatively unorthodox, he was one of the best teachers for me. There is a classic example that I often tell to illustrate this.

In my freshman year of university I took an arranging class with this unusual teacher. The goal of the class was to write eight bars of music per week so at the end of the semester the students would have a completed work. Well, I had such a driving passion for writing music, that I wrote one or two *completed* arrangements *per week!* He told me, many years later, that he *still* remembered the awe and wonder in my eyes when I heard the music I had written played for the first time, turning to him and saying, regarding my future, "This is what I want to do." Well aware by then of my great love and passion for writing music, and the potential in the music I was writing, he became my mentor, so to speak, and I a protégé.

He was a really great arranger and jazz pianist, and I would sometimes go to his office to hang out with him to talk or listen to him play the piano. One day after teaching one of his classes, he came back to his office and sat and started playing one of the standard American songs that had become part of the jazz repertoire, but was substituting the original harmony with his own alternate chord changes, and they were absolutely *beautiful.* Every time he changed from one chord to something even more exquisite, he'd look over at me through his round, John Lennon-type glasses, like he wanted to make sure that I understood what he was trying to say about the meaning, the essence and beauty of the alternate harmony. I sat staring back with reverent amazement, silently acknowledging that I did have a sense of understanding, and that I wanted to learn more. And when it seemed he had reached the apogee of what he was trying to get across to me, he suddenly stopped playing. He then slowly turned toward me, and looking straight into my eyes like he was trusting me with the secret of the universe, he spread the fingers of both of his hands in front of him, locking the index finger of the bottom hand with the pinky of his upper hand, and said, in a very cool jazz vernacular, "Colors man . . . colors." That was it! That simple hand gesture that symbolized the mixing of orchestral voices, and *one word,* "colors," contained everything that one needed to know of the deep ocean of knowledge he was trying to impart.

Again, twenty-five years later, with all my years of studying Eastern philosophy from which to draw from, I told him that he had actually been like a modern American Zen Master and I his disciple, because he was able to sum up *everything* with just one word: "colors." We both had a really good laugh about it, but it was in fact very true. If the student "got it," fine. And if not, that was fine too because that's all there was. From that point on it was up to the student to learn what it meant. Believe me, I still ponder over its deep meaning and significance, learning more with every note I write. Now *that* is education.

The other thing that made school worth it was the special friendships that grew. Just like in the professional world, it is the people we come up the ranks with that often times help us later on in our professional life. Hopefully we can help one another. For some, school offers a safe and structured environment in which to meet people and "network." For many it is the boot camp of the real world, and in that way can be very beneficial for those who need it as a stepping stone to the professional world, socially as well as creatively. It's a very personal decision, though. School might be the perfect choice for some, and a waste of time and money for another. All I can add is that in the professional music world, and I would imagine in the professional art world in general, people could care less where you went to school and how many degrees you have. All they care about is, *can you play? Can you write? Can you paint? Can you dance? Can you create?* And if you are easy to get along with it also helps a lot. We're not here alone. All of our successes are a collaboration of some kind. We need people and must be able to get along well with others as best we can.

We live in such a different world now though. Of the generations before mine, so many of the people who attained *huge* success never got past a high school education, if that. They learned as they went along and maximized what they had to work with: their talent, imagination, and resourcefulness, which are much more important in life than a wall full of degrees. *Now*, unfortunately, depending on what you hope to do as your life's work, no matter how talented you are, you are most likely not going to be given the time of day if you don't have a minimum of a four-year university degree, and even that is no longer impressive. It seems you need a minimum of a masters degree. And what I find rather ridiculous is that in order to teach at most universities one needs a doctorate. A doctorate is no guarantee of *anything* other than someone spent a whole lot of years in school. That is no indication that one is a great teacher, a great leader, or has the ability to succeed themselves in the professional world outside of academia. How can one train others to succeed in the "real world" when many doctoral degree holders in the arts, for example, have not attained even the slightest measure of professional success? How could they? They've never gotten out of school. Obtaining a doctorate can be a great accomplishment that one can be very proud of. It certainly has its merit. And in some academic disciplines, especially where analysis or the study of history is involved, the kind of education that pursuing a doctorate can provide, might actually be mandatory in order to gain the wealth of knowledge required to teach such subjects. But concerning the creative arts, I think Einstein's words sum up my sentiments very simply: "The only source of knowledge is experience." A woman once told me, with a kind of proud arrogance, that her son was working on a doctoral degree in composition, and I thought to myself, "that's probably a good indication that he cannot *really* write music at all," because in the words of French composer Louise Talma, "Too many composers become involved in intellectual speculation which seems to matter more than the sound that comes out of all the speculation." This applies not only to composition, but also to any artistic endeavor.

However, I happen to know several *wonderful* educators who have doctoral degrees in music. In fact, one of my favorite conductors, who is very active in the professional world, not only has a doctorate, he was also Chairman of the music department at the University of California, Los Angeles. There do exist educators with higher degrees who have their hands in both the academic and professional worlds and do both with excellence. My issue is not with the degree holders or the degree itself. My issue is with institutionalized education's arrogant exclusion of many absolutely *brilliant* and inspired people who have already attained the very success that the instructors are attempting to help their students to achieve. But because they do not hold a particular degree they are banished from the halls of so-called "higher learning." What sense does *that* make? What kind of "education" has lead to that kind of twisted logic? This mentality is yet another example of the elitist, prejudicial nonsense that is based on arbitrary rules that stand as the pillars that uphold an ineffective system of education, where academic credentials have become more important than the very life experience and knowledge that school is supposed to help one achieve. Of course academia is valuable to some extent but *not* to the degree that such exaggerated importance is placed on it, and to the exclusion of what is most important: a *balanced* education. A lifetime of experience and success is worth more than a hundred doctoral degrees. There is no substitute for experience and no substitute for success. Just keep all of this in mind when deciding *for yourself* what the best path of "education" is for you.

> "Education is a wonderful thing, provided you always remember that nothing worth knowing can ever be taught."
>
> Oscar Wilde
> Irish playwright

Education Quotations

Education Quotations

"Nothing in education is so astonishing as the amount of ignorance it accumulates in the form of facts."

Henry Adams
American writer and historian

"Analysis kills spontaneity. The grain once ground into flour springs and germinates no more."

Henri Frederic Amiel
Swiss writer and philosopher

"It is possible to store the mind with a million facts and still be entirely uneducated."

Alec Bourne
Author

"A loving heart is the beginning of all knowledge."

Thomas Carlyle
Scottish essayist, historian, and philosopher

"Education is what remains after one has forgotten everything he learned in school."

Albert Einstein
German-born American physicist

"Creative minds have always been known to survive any kind of bad training."

Anna Freud
British psychoanalyst

"The aim of education is the knowledge not of fact, but of values."

Dean William R. Inge
Author and religious leader

"It is a thousand times better to have common sense without education than to have education without common sense."

Robert Green Ingersoll
Orator and political speechmaker

"Education is not the filling of a pail, but the lighting of a fire."

William Butler Yeats
Irish poet, dramatist, and mystic

Creativity and a Loving Spirit

Chapter Four
Creativity and a Loving Spirit

"Neither a lofty degree of intelligence nor imagination
nor both together go to the making of genius.
Love, love, love, that is the soul of genius."
Wolfgang Amadeus Mozart
Austrian composer

Love is such a tremendous catalyst for creativity. I cannot think of anything that is greater or more powerful. Think of all the beautiful songs written because of someone's inspired love for another; all the music through the ages, the poetry, the paintings. What about all the grand iconic structures like the Taj Mahal for example, that were made to symbolize the depth of one's love for another? How about all the courageous and creatively heroic deeds done in the name of love; the bravery, the chivalry that changed the course of history? Love, no doubt, is pretty powerful stuff. *Of course* it is a tremendous catalyst for creativity: *It is the source of creativity.*

What does love do in a creative way?

- It gives us the strength and courage to take risks.
- It helps us to endure in order to see our creative vision through.
- It helps us to commit without compromise.
- It helps us to materialize all that we need.

- It gives us a sense of purpose and knowingness as to why we are here.
- It helps us to determine our creative direction.
- It helps us to connect with all of creation on a deep level.
- It helps us to understand the underlying "oneness" of all things.
- It creates miracles.

How do love and creativity affect people?

- They heal.
- They transform.
- They uplift.
- They inspire.
- They give hope.
- They give us courage.
- They help us to have good self-esteem and self-worth.
- They allow us to see and experience the Divinity in ourselves and others.
- They create peace.

For me, love, in its many facets of expression, is the only thing worth living for because a life without love is no life at all. A life without love is death, creatively and otherwise. English poet Robert Browning said, "Take away love and our Earth is a tomb." To not love and be loved is to not truly be alive. Yet there seems to be much confusion about what love really is. In an article, "How We Learn to Develop Genuine Love," it states: "Genuine love is more than just affection or sentiment. It consistently acts in the very best interests of others, even if they do not fully appreciate it at the time, which is often the case . . ."[38] It is love that helps us find ourselves, helps us develop to our full potential and evolve to a higher state of awareness and understanding. It is love that motivates us to do things that literally change the world and transform a place of ugliness into a place of beauty. And it is love that can mend a broken heart and breathe life into the lifeless. The article goes on to say, "A medical researcher wrote: 'Love and intimacy are at a root of what makes us sick and what makes us well, what causes sadness and what brings happiness, what makes us suffer and what leads to healing. If a new drug had the same impact, virtually every doctor in the country would be recommending it for their patients. It would be malpractice not to prescribe it.'"[39]

Love is infinite. However, despite its infinite vastness, it is in the small details of everything we do that the quality, depth, and power of our love materializes and becomes so apparent. Mother Theresa's words echo this truth: "Be faithful in small things because it is in them that your strength lies." Caring about those seemingly small details speaks volumes about who we are, and what is of greatest importance to us. Because it takes such great love and *attention* to care about all the little things, they make the greatest impact and bring the most positive results. A great seer of India said, "You are where your attention takes you. In fact, you are your attention."[40] If our attention is firmly focused on love, and all that it encompasses, then we are love and everything we do will be a vivid expression of its beauty and power. When our intentions and way of living are deeply rooted in love and truth, then paying honor and attention to the small details is not a hardship. It is an effortless joy, one of our greatest rewards. It becomes as natural as breathing, a reflex, a spontaneous outpouring of the poetry written in the code of love within every cell of our being. For example, this could be remembering all the little things that please those we love, letting them know how much we love them without their having to prompt us or there having to be a special occasion or reason; a gentle and tender touch of reassurance, paying full attention, truly listening. These are just a few of the simple ways to honor the Divinity in someone we love. This same loving attention to detail also applies to other aspects of our creative expression. It's what makes the difference between good and *great*; competent and *inspired*; adequate and *transforming*. Truly caring about the quality and integrity of every detail of our work has great power, and that power literally becomes infused into everything that we do, touching others on both a conscious and subconscious level.

Composing music is one of the important ways I am able to express my love and creativity in this life. It has become effortless and spontaneous. So too is the compassion and concern I feel for both the musicians who breathe life into those dots of intention and potentiality (the music), and also the listeners. I ask myself, "Is the composition too long-winded and self-absorbed? Can I say what I feel my soul needs to say in a way and length that shows compassion for the attention span and comfort level of the audience as well as the musicians (the concept of less being more), without feeling I have compromised its quality and true meaning? The following quote of composer Igor Stravinsky supports my feelings about this: "Too many pieces of music finish too long after the end." I also ask myself, *Is the actual music manuscript presented to the individual musicians in its most visually pleasing form? Will it help them to feel comfortable and happy? Is it easy on their eyes as well as easy to read? Do the individually written parts visually represent the spirit of the music?* For example, if the music evokes a feeling of spaciousness and vastness, is the actual music manuscript presented to each musician, written in such a way that helps them to not only feel that vastness, but also *see* the picture the music is trying to paint? Or in order to save money, is everything crunched together requiring fewer pages, but losing the desired visual affect and emotional response? Is everything presented with love?

I care about *every detail*. It makes a difference. It makes a *huge* difference in the effect the music has on both the audience and musicians whether they are consciously aware of it or not. All the better if they are, but I trust that at minimum, the subconscious takes it all in and responds accordingly. The music is played differently as a result of the loving care that is put into its creation and presentation. It is played with more depth and more beauty. The audience receives it more willingly and more lovingly. They feel and understand the music at a deeper level without having to be read a long explanation about what it means or having to actually be an educated musician to understand and embrace it. And when the music is infused with this kind of love, something rather miraculous occurs that makes the performance and overall experience much greater and much more meaningful than it would have otherwise been: the form and technicalities of the music are superceded by the love put into every detail, merging the audience, the musicians, and the music itself into one unified whole, one body of love speaking and understanding the same language. I have experienced this over and over again. This is my truth. This is love: love for the music, love for the musicians, love for the audience, love for myself, love for the whole world.

We have a responsibility to the audience. And contrary to the popular belief of many of those in the arts, to be thoughtful toward the audience *does not* hinder our originality, but only enhances our creativity through the loving feedback loop we have created. In a particular reference to writing poetry, American Poet Laureate Ted Kooser articulated this beautifully in his wonderful book, *The Poetry Home Repair Manual:* "I believe with all my heart that it is a virtue to show our appreciation for readers by writing with kindness, generosity and humility toward them."[41]

We must always keep in mind how important our audience is. Without an audience of some kind to experience our work, the creative equation is incomplete. It's a reciprocal arrangement, one of sharing. We need each other. Without an audience, it's very much the same as experiencing unrequited love. Yes, we can just enjoy the process ourselves, but to *really* experience its full and deeper meaning, the fruits of our creativity, like love, must be shared. According to the fascinating information that is part of the New Physics, such as Heisenberg's Uncertainty Principle, "the observer alters the observed by the mere act of observation."[42] Taking this a step further, "Princeton physicist John A. Wheeler believes that the term 'observer' should be replaced by the term 'participator'."[43] So, we have a collaboration happening with our audience that seems to go very deep, having a very interconnected and mystical quality to it. Somehow the "observer," or audience, plays a very important role in the creations we bring to life in more ways than we might have ever imagined.

Perhaps this third-dimensional experience we are having here is a kind of "proving ground" of the universe that prepares us for a more refined, elegant, and truly loving way of living, being, and creating. Maybe it is through the grace and integrity we display under such difficult and challenging circumstances here, that we transform to a more subtle and elegant level of vibration, which helps us to move on to a life of love and creativity both here and in the hereafter.

> "In our life, there is a single color, as on an artist's palette, which provides the meaning of life and art. It is the color of love."
>
> Marc Chagall
> Russian-born French painter

Love Quotations

Love Quotations

"Love is a great beautifier."

Louisa May Alcott
American novelist

"The best proof of love is trust."

Dr. Joyce Brothers
American psychologist, TV-radio personality, and author

"Where there is great love there are always miracles."

Willa Cather
American journalist and novelist

"Love is always creative, fear always destructive."

Emmet Fox
Scientist, philosopher, spiritual teacher, and author

"To love what you do and feel that it matters—how could anything be more fun?"

Katherine Graham
American publisher and author

"I don't wish to be everything to everyone, but I would like to be something to someone."

Javan
American poet

"I was created in love. For that reason nothing can express my beauty nor liberate me except love alone."

Mechtild of Magdeburg
Medieval mystic

"It is not the magnitude of our actions but the amount of love that is put into them that matters."

Mother Teresa
20th Century humanitarian

"At the touch of love, everyone becomes a poet."

Plato
Greek philosopher

"To the world you may be one person, but to one person you may be the world."

Bill Wilson
Founder of Alcoholics Anonymous

Creativity and Relationship

Chapter Five
Creativity and Relationship

"Are we not like two volumes of one book?"
Marceline Desbordes-Valmore
French poet

What I learned from the Sufi mystic Hazrat Inayat Khan about love, harmony, and vibration, is that it is not sound or color alone that are harmonious or inharmonious, but the relationship of one sound with another, or one color and another that creates harmony or disharmony.[44] Two people, two notes, or two colors may be just fine as individuals, but the combination of the two can be either expansive or destructive, pleasing or offensive, beautiful or ugly, depending on the chemistry, the way the two vibratory forces interact. This applies to all aspects of life where relationships of any kind are concerned. Will the combination create harmony that is pleasing and healing or bring about an unsettling dissonance? The answer seems to be found in the physics of vibration.

Everything in the universe is vibrating.[45] *We* are vibrating. We often talk about getting a "vibe" *from* someone or "vibing" *with* someone or something: music, a poem, a work of art, or even a concept or idea. The degree to which we can feel these vibrations depends on how evolved our sensory perception is. And since everything is vibrating, that means everything is a wave. Learning this helped me to understand that no matter how well I am living my life, from time to time there are still going to be ups and downs no matter what. So I don't question myself so harshly anymore when I feel I'm doing everything "right" yet occasionally things seem to go wrong. Now I know that it doesn't necessarily have anything to do with me. And knowing this reassures me that if I feel I'm in the trough, the low point of the wave, the way of the universe guarantees that I will also be able to ride the crest once again. That's just the nature of waves.

Life is certainly an adventure ride, and I guess in one way or another we're all surfing the universe trying to catch the exciting waves of life with the hope of riding them safely to shore without wiping out. And although we sometimes feel tossed around by the ups and downs, our attitude toward the experience can play a very important role in smoothing things out to where the ups and downs are not as extreme, allowing us to glide through the difficult times knowing that "this too shall pass."

At any given stage of our evolution, we are vibrating at a frequency that reflects that level of evolution, and attracts to us the music, sounds, colors, situations, and people that are of a similar vibration. If we are not very spiritually evolved, we generate and attract lower density vibrations. And likewise, if we are farther along in our spiritual evolution, we vibrate at a higher frequency and need to surround ourselves with people and things that are more suitable to our higher self in order to feel comfortable and continue growing. As our frequency changes, we may no longer resonate or "vibe" with the people we once felt comfortable being around. And they may not be able to tune us in anymore, because just as a radio with a certain sensitivity is required in order to tune in to certain stations, a person no longer equipped to receive our higher frequency is not going to be able to "hear" us. They won't understand us. And sometimes they will even resent us for our growth because it doesn't include them going along for the ride, or at least it seems so on the surface. Likewise, we may not want to tune in to the old stations whose programs are no longer suitable or of interest to us, preferring the new music and information being broadcast on new channels whose frequencies are higher and signals clearer. Don't feel bad about outgrowing things and people. It is an unavoidable part of life. It's OK. It doesn't mean we don't care about them or appreciate the role they once played in helping us grow, keeping us company as we traveled a phase of our life's journey.

Fortunately, there *are* those who will go the distance with us, but not everyone evolves at the same rate and we shouldn't inhibit our own growth or the growth of others because of this sometimes-uncomfortable reality. In a similar way, we also shouldn't feel guilty about leaving older aspects of our creative expression behind, because they too may no longer serve us well. We need to try new things and express ourselves in new ways, constantly growing, constantly evolving. Sometimes, though, people who like our work as is, and expect more of the same, might not be too comfortable with the changes. That's OK too. But as our frequency changes, many of our needs change. Just continue to follow your truth. Follow your bliss. Everything else has a way of falling into place.

While writing the composition *Gates of Gold* in 1993, I had a revelation about love, relationship, and counterpoint in music. Counterpoint is the marriage of independent melodies or parts, fashioned in a way so as to enhance each other and bring out their respective beauty, strength, personality and uniqueness without suppressing or overshadowing the other. At its best, each one helps the other to shine, to develop, and live to its full potential, to be clearly heard, and to have meaning. This is how true love is. This is what a marriage or any loving relationship should be: two seemingly separate people coming together for a common purpose of creating one body of love. If the love is true, it rejoices in the successes of the other and celebrates as if it were their own. From the interplay of this cosmic counterpoint, new life is created in one form or another, and often a new motif that develops its own unique melody is created within that body and love gives birth to more love. Each phase of a relationship is like the movements of life's symphony that, if well written, performed with excellence and integrity, and conducted with care and commanding guidance, will hopefully lead to a glorious finale.

So much can be learned about life through music. Both the simple and the intricate inner workings within the body of a composition and in an ensemble itself are so reflective of the dynamics of everyday relationships on all levels: the highs and lows, the soft and loud, the harmony and dissonance. There is a rhythm, a pulse that gives life to a composition and carries it from its first breath to its final rest. It has a heart and soul. I am often given some wonderful revelations about life and relationship through music. One such metaphoric revelation involves what, in music, are called *suspensions*. A suspension occurs when one note of a chord is delayed, prolonging the return of the chord to its root, or "home" position, which gives the feeling of resolution or completion. Peace. To put it simply, the movement is one of *tension and release*. I was wondering why I had always been so attracted to the beauty of suspensions, and then I suddenly had an "A-Ha" moment: *this is life*. Tension and release, tension and release, tension and release. The resolved chord seems to have more beauty because of the tension that preceded it. Now we're right back to what I mentioned in the Introduction: no light without darkness, no happiness without sadness, no pleasure without pain. Everything in life is about relationship. This is the music of life.

> "To preserve your relationship to nature, make your life more moral, more pure, more innocent."
>
> Henry David Thoreau
> American philosopher and naturalist

Relationship Quotations

Relationship Quotations

"Nothing is more exciting and bonding in relationships than creating together."

Stephen Covey
American author

"I felt it shelter to speak to you."

Emily Dickenson
American poet

"Who you are speaks so loudly I can't hear what you're saying."

Ralph Waldo Emerson
American philosopher, essayist, and lecturer

"People who generate similar frequencies are attracted to each other, resulting in friendship. When frequencies are fundamentally incompatible, they cannot resonate."[46]

Masaru Emoto
Japanese author and doctor of alternative medicine

"Remember, we all stumble, every one of us. That's why it's a comfort to go hand in hand."

Emily Kimbrough
American writer

"Knowing how to yield is strength."

Lao Tzu
Chinese philosopher and founder of Taoism

"The most terrible poverty is loneliness and the feeling of being unloved."

Mother Teresa
20th Century humanitarian

"The quality of your life is the quality of your relationships."

Anthony Robbins
American motivational speaker and writer

"Self-respect and a clear conscience are powerful components of integrity and are the basis for enriching your relationships with others."

Denis Waitley
American personal development expert

Creativity and Music

Chapter Six
Creativity and Music

"In music alone we see God free from all forms and thoughts.
It is because music is the picture of our Beloved that we love music."
Hazrat Inayat Khan
Sufi mystic, musician, author

I have chosen to discuss music in particular, because it is the form
of creativity that I have the most experience with. Not only that, I
believe that art, poetry, photography, dance, knitting, sewing, cooking,
gardening, flying, and every other expression of creativity are forms
of music, love, and relationship.

Regarding the work of a composer, in its truest and most spiritually
supreme form, Sufi mystic Hazrat Inayat Khan said,

> "A composer of music performs his small part in the
> scheme of nature as creator. Music being the most
> exalted of arts, the work of the composer of music is
> no less than the work of a saint." [17]

At this point in my own personal, spiritual, and artistic evolution
as a composer of music, I find that my sources of inspiration are very
different than they were in previous years, which were found in the

typically imagined forms, such as listening to other music, studying music books or the musical scores of other composers, or going to concerts, all of which have been important at some point along my path. I still enjoy such things from time to time, but they are no longer where I find my greatest inspiration. For me the source of inspiration may be the elusive beauty of silence, or the changing colors of the sky after a storm, when fingers of golden light reach through the clouds and touch the face of the sea. It could be the lonely chill in the air as I walk a dimly lit street, kicking the leaves whose spectrum of beauty intensifies as they prepare to rest after a life well-lived. Or it can be in holding the hand of the one I love, where no words need be spoken to have the most passionate love poetry recited to my heart. How lovely it is to be able to find music in the most seemingly surprising but supremely metaphoric places. This is my personal experience now, composing music.

I never really sit down and say, "Today I'm going to write such and such . . ." I may think about what I might like to write if and when the right time presents itself, but I have found it most beneficial to not impose myself upon the music, to keep myself out of the way and allow it to unfold at its proper time. I am often inspired by a poetic title that has come to my heart and mind and I think, *How nice it would be to write something based on that.* So, I add it to the list of titles that I keep, and then make my intentions known to the universe with a pure heart and pure motives, but letting go of my attachment to the outcome. When its time does arrive, it's as if I'm tapped on the shoulder and the composition says, "Excuse me, but it's time to be born." It is at that moment that basically everything is presented effortlessly: the themes and shape of the composition, all the colors and shades of the orchestration, which instruments should play a given part at a given time, and a basic glimpse of the whole before one note is written on paper. I can even see individual musicians and how they move their arms, how they breathe just a fraction of a moment before they send their lifeforce soaring on its mystical journey through the twists and turns of their beloved instruments; the synchronized ballet of bows rising and falling in unison, gliding in formation across a taut lake of aural glass. Emotionally, the experience is a kind of pastel wash, an atmosphere of soft colors that embraces me. My biggest challenge at that point is trying to keep up with the flow of energy and information, which is usually very rapid and overwhelmingly intense.

During this creative unfolding, time ceases to exist and hours can feel like the blink of an eye. I look at what has just been created with a kind of wonder and disbelief, knowing that somehow I was part of the process, but not the source of the information. I feel more like a channel for the music. It came *through* me and I just notated it and colored it with my spirit. I feel the very best of what I have done in music, the compositions that seem to move people the most, were a product of this kind of "channeling" experience; however, this has not always been the case. Although music has always come relatively effortlessly for me, I still labored long hours, completely immersed in its beauty, learning the craft of writing music, and exploring the many facets of my creativity. And it was this earlier form of creative discovery that lead to the current experience I'm now having in music, both experiences having proven to be very valuable aspects of the overall creative equation in my life.

The legendary German composer Ludwig van Beethoven said, "Music is a higher revelation than all wisdom and philosophy," and English writer Aldous Huxley wrote, "After silence, that which comes nearest to expressing the inexpressible is music." For me, music is the purest form of love that I have ever known, and maybe that's all I need to know.

"Of all the music that reached farthest into heaven, it
is the beating of a loving heart."

Henry Ward Beecher
American preacher and reformer

Music Quotations

Music Quotations

"Music is well said to be the speech of angels; in fact, nothing among the utterances allowed to man is felt to be so divine. It brings us near to the infinite."

Thomas Carlyle
Scottish essayist, historian, and philosopher

"Don't play what's there, play what's not there."

Miles Davis
American musician

"The truest expression of a people is in its dances and its music."

Agnes De Mille
American choreographer

"The world may consist of musical notes as well as of mathematical rules."

Albert Einstein
German-born American physicist

"Music expresses that which cannot be put into words and that which cannot remain silent."

Victor Hugo
French novelist

"Music makes more people milder and gentler, more moral and more reasonable."

Martin Luther
German reformation leader

"I rock—therefore I am."

Parker McGee
American songwriter

"Music creates order out of chaos: for rhythm imposes unanimity upon the divergent, melody imposes continuity upon the disjointed, and harmony imposes compatibility upon the incongruous."

Yehudi Menuhin
American violinist

"There is nothing in the world so much like prayer as music is."

William P. Merrill
American pastor

"Without music, life would be a mistake."

Friedrich Nietzsche
German philosopher

Creativity and Silence

Chapter Seven
Creativity and Silence

"One of the greatest sounds of them all—
and to me it is a sound—
is utter, complete silence."

Andre Kostelanetz
Russian-born American pianist, conductor, and arranger

When my experience with music and life made a huge shift in 1993 and started having a very mystical quality, silence suddenly became exquisitely beautiful. Not only did it become beautiful *and* inspiring, it became *crucial* to my existence and creative expression, as well as to my happiness and comfort. Suddenly I was hearing things that I never noticed before in ways that I never would have imagined, both for better and for worse. The sound of the wind and trees became completely intoxicating to me, yet I also felt totally assaulted by a cacophony of disturbing sounds all around me that began rattling every cell of my body to the core: car alarms, cell-phones, beepers, leaf blowers, lawn mowers, garbage trucks, traffic, car horns, "music" pounding and blaring from cars, etc. I mean, if the powerful low-frequency vibrations of a passing garbage truck can set off car alarms, then it's no wonder why it makes *me* so miserably uncomfortable. High frequencies as well have an effect on both our mood and physical health, and there is an increasing amount of well-documented evidence to prove that.

In his book *Leap of Faith,* one of the original Mercury Seven
astronauts, Gordon Cooper, discusses the harmful affects of both
Extremely Low Frequencies (ELF), and high frequencies on humans
and animals. He stated that, "Anything above 11 Hertz (cycles per
second) produced a general agitation or uneasiness."[48] Considering
that high voltage power lines emit 50 to 60 Hz, there is need then, for
serious concern regarding the potential health hazards that these high
frequency emissions are having on humans and animals. I have both
read of, and seen documentaries that brought this concern to light.
Electromagnetic radiation is a harmful environmental pollutant linked
to cancer and various diseases. People who live near high voltage power
lines suffer from a high rate of leukemia, and there are many accounts
of people suffering a variety of disabilities thought to be caused by
stray voltage from Extra Low Frequency power lines.[49] One
documentary showed the mild, but continual electrocution of cattle
from stray voltage on a dairy farm situated near such power lines.

On the positive side, Cooper goes on to say that frequencies under
7 Hz create a very blissful state in us known as the "alpha state," with
the most beneficial frequency on Earth believed to be 6.8 Hz. Is it just
a coincidence that the Cheops Pyramid has been found to have a
constant 6.8 Hz signal running through it?[50] I hardly think so. Though
experts are still unaware of its source, considering all the other mystical
aspects and mysteries surrounding this ancient Egyptian pyramid, we
should not be surprised.

We are electromagnetic energy and electricity can kill us or jolt us
back to life. It can energize or calm us. It can agitate or cause depression
in human beings. There's a very fragile balance involved. If a low
frequency signal can even penetrate the copper-lined walls of a Faraday
cage,[51] just imagine what they can do to us. The genius inventor Nikola
Tesla had experimented with very low frequencies and his original
notes alluded to specific good and bad psychological affects that these
frequencies could produce. There is well-documented evidence of
ELFs being used to affect whole populations, including the widespread

death of cattle in Oregon, which was concluded to be the result of ELFs that were being transmitted by the Russians.[52] This was known in intelligence circles as "Woodpecker."[53] Seventy-five years earlier, Tesla had upset radio communications around the world as a result of his experiments with ELFs and many countries filed protests.[54] These are just a few examples that attest to the potentially disruptive and destructive power of "noise." And, as you can hopefully see, there are different kinds of noise, so it is no wonder that, depending on our level of sensitivity and what we can withstand, noise is in fact a form of pollution and toxicity that can greatly affect our well-being, upsetting both our emotional and chemical balance.

Once my life began making the transformation that it did, my ability to withstand noise had decreased dramatically. I started to wonder if I was beginning to lose my mind. But the following quote of philosopher Arthur Schopenhauer, that I fortunately found soon after this sensitivity to noise began, reassured me that I hadn't gone completely crazy: "The amount of noise which anyone can bear undisturbed stands in inverse proportion to his mental capacity . . . Nature shows that with the growth of intelligence comes increased capacity for pain, and it is only with the highest degree of intelligence that suffering reaches its supreme point." And more recently, something I read by sound healer and author Steve Halpern seemed as if it was explaining my new experience with noise very accurately: "In twentieth-century society, the noise level is such that it keeps knocking our bodies out of tune and out of their natural rhythms. This ever-increasing assault of sounds upon our ears, mind, and bodies adds to the stress load of civilized beings trying to live in a highly complex environment."

One of the interesting things about sensitivity is that when we become more sensitive, it's a package deal: we become more sensitive to the fineness of beauty but also to all the ugliness around us, the selfishness, unkindness, and cruelty. Sounds and experiences that were, I guess, previously just background noise in the soundtrack of my life, that my conscious mind must have tuned out, suddenly became deafening torment and a shocking assault on my body, mind, and spirit. But likewise as my sensitivity and general awareness began expanding, so many lovely things that had gone completely unnoticed before suddenly seemed to materialize out of nowhere. And the simplest expressions of thoughtfulness and kindness became permanently etched on the tablet of my heart and infused into everything I would do, say, or think from then on. The gentlest sound became the most Divine music in the universe to me, and all I had to do to receive it was just be still and listen . . .

But that has become quite a challenge in today's noisy world. Besides the bombardment of noise from heavy machinery, the sophisticated toys of technology, and the assault of high and low frequencies all around us, I have noticed that there is just too much chatter in the world. There is too much talking and not enough listening. I'm quite tired of being forced to listen to so many conversations that I wish I could totally tune out. As a result of the great amount of forced exposure to this seemingly endless blur of blabbing that I have to suffer through, I have come to the conclusion that this plague of people constantly talking on cell phones, for example, is an indication of the loneliness and detachment they are experiencing in the disintegrating social structure in which we live. To compensate, people are constantly on their cell-phones, unconsciously trying to stay connected in a very disconnected world. One would think that the convenience of cell-phones and e-mail would ease this loneliness and isolation, but I think they have actually made it worse. They are a bit *too* convenient and this convenience has robbed us of the time that could be devoted to quiet self-reflection and introspection, as well as further separating us from one another by reducing the efforts we used to make to meet in person, to gather in person to share. For the most part, there is no "village" anymore, other than becoming a coffee-zombie, and even in coffee places it's difficult to hear oneself think with all the loud cell phone conversations that echo through the cavernous "warehouse chic" architecture. The idea of such a gathering place is a good start in our attempts to reintegrate, but it looks like the same unhealthy elements have just been transferred from one place to another. This detachment and alienation has even infiltrated the world of "love" relationships, devolving into cyber-relationships. I refuse to fuel such a warped arrangement because detachment on *that* level just leads to destruction and heartache. Whatever happened to touch and looking into the eyes of someone we love?

Everyone seems too busy now to spend time together, and so the feelings of alienation are increasing to epidemic proportions. This has become a kind of social sickness that creates an unhealthy and continuous barrage of noise that seems to never stop no matter where we go. Even when I try to go to the park for quiet, invariably there is someone yakking up a storm on their cell-phone, discussing the stock market, or complaining about their mate. I would like to ask them what the point is of their being in the park because it's obvious that they are missing it:

> "There is always music amongst the trees of the garden, but our hearts must be very quiet to hear it."
>
> M. Aumonier

And "nature" is not exempt from the general imbalance that is happening on this planet. The ecological system is so compromised from pollution, urbanization, and the loss of natural habitat, that it seems too many species of birds and animals are fighting for the same small territory. The dense concentration of all of them in one place causes a deafening cacophony that I find unbearable at times. The streets are literally *littered* with crows in the area in which I live. This wasn't the case ten years ago. The whole balance of life is *way off* and silence is one of the biggest casualties. Each of us must do what we can to help restore balance to our world, and silence is a good place to start.

> "Let us be silent that we may hear the whispers of the gods."
>
> Ralph Waldo Emerson

It is in the *silence*, in the space between our thoughts, that we find the answers to our prayers, but we need to be still enough to be able to hear those answers. That requires turning down all the various forms of "noise" in our life. Having a quiet mind helps us find the gems of love and creativity that can easily get lost among all the rubble that clutters our hearts and minds. How each of us accomplishes this is very personal, but somehow we must find some moments every day to be still in our own respective ways and just listen quietly to the rapturous fullness of the silence. Although in the world we live, it might seem a near impossibility or a luxury to take a few moments to be still every day, it is crucial to our physical, mental, and spiritual well-being that we do so. Our creative health and growth greatly rests upon our ability to create an atmosphere of peace and tranquility in which we can then hear the voices of our hearts. If we cannot afford a few moments of quiet and self-reflection every day, then I believe it is indication enough that our lives are out of balance and need adjusting. It is an expression of faith and trust in ourselves and our Higher Power, to take the time for quiet and self-reflection, without fear.

As a composer of music, it is in the silence that I can hear the Universe orchestrating itself. The Divine fullness and richness of one note, just *one note* ringing, becomes a symphony in itself. I want to listen to all it has to say, become immersed in its aural ocean and bathe in its waves before moving on to the next note, each note being its own world, having its own personality, its own color, its own story to tell. I experienced this most vividly when composing "Heaven and Earth" from the CD *The Music of Life*. By allowing the notes *and* the silence between the notes of the unfolding composition to ring, giving them space and time, a rich rainbow of overtones hung suspended in the air, beautifully orchestrating the composition with simplicity and perfection. There was nothing for me to do except stay out of the way and give the music all the space it needed. This sensitivity to space and silence was the key that opened a cosmic door to more "other-dimensional," non-local kinds of extrasensory experiences with music.

When I walk into a quiet, empty room, I sense the ether filled with melodies searching to be born. That quiet room becomes the "otherworld" where these transformed melodic souls, who have been reflecting in another frequency, are there waiting to materialize once again, having chosen me as the channel, the conduit through whom their new life will blossom. In a way, we become collaborators who have made an agreement to bring beauty to life together. I have been searching for them and they have been waiting for me. All I have to do is just show up with a pure heart, a quiet mind, and the best of intentions, along with a joyful willingness to welcome these melodies, these loving, living beings to the world.

"Heard melodies are sweet, but those unheard are sweeter."

John Keats
English poet

Silence Quotations

Silence Quotations

"A man who lives right, and is right, has more power in his silence that another has by his words."

Phillips Brooks
American clergyman and author

"He is nearest to the gods who knows how to be silent."

Marcus Porcius Cato
Roman statesman

"The mass gross absence of sound in space is more than just silence."

Eugene Cernan
Apollo 17 Astronaut, author, and last man on the moon

"In the attitude of silence the soul finds the path in a clearer light, and what is elusive and deceptive resolves itself into crystal clearness."

Mahatma Gandhi
Indian spiritual and political leader

"Silence is the element in which great things fashion themselves."

Count Maurice Maeterlinck
Belgian poet, dramatist, and essayist

"All men's miseries derive from not being able to sit quiet in a room alone."

Blaise Pascal
French mathematician, philosopher, and physicist

"Silence is the language of the realized. Practice moderation in speech; that will help you in many ways."

Sai Baba
Indian spiritual teacher

"The pauses between the notes . . . ah, that is where the art resides!"

Artur Schnabel
Polish-born American classical pianist

"The beginning of wisdom is silence. The second step is listening."

Unknown Author

Creativity and Intuition

Chapter Eight
Creativity and Intuition

"Intuition is a spiritual faculty and does not explain,
but simply points the way."

Florence Scovel Shinn
American artist and metaphysics teacher

I have heard it said that we'd be much better off trusting our "gut" because, unlike our mind, our "gut" has not evolved to the point of having self-doubt.[55] It's a pretty accurate indicator of what would be best for us, before our intellect gets in the way with all its defensiveness and wayward issues. Einstein stated, "The intellect has little to do on the road to discovery. There comes a leap in consciousness, call it intuition or what you will, and the solution comes to you and you don't know how or why."

Intuition is the raw data, the uncensored truth that blossoms from the infinite library of knowledge deep within our subconscious, and gives us the insights to discern the true nature of things. It is the omnipresent Divine intelligence that permeates every aspect of our bodymind. It is our faithful and unfailing guide that lets us know where to go and what to do without analysis or intellectualization. We derive the direction we need through hunches, insights, "feelings," twinges in our "gut," and messages our body sends us in a variety of ways. Our intuition allows us to follow a path without consciously knowing the way, yet somehow knowing it's correct. It is an inexplicable "knowingness," a kind of extra-sensory perception. It gives us a clear picture of "the whole" of a situation in an instant and allows us to make a snap decision in that fraction of a moment. In the words of Nobel Laureate in medicine and physiology, Alex Carrel, "Intuition comes very close to clairvoyance; it appears to be the extrasensory perception of reality." Our bodies are intelligent. Every cell is a thinking cell that is constantly sharing information with one another.[56] It helps to listen to our body for the answers. It tells the truth.

Regarding the body's wisdom, English writer D.H. Lawrence wrote, "The mind can assert anything and pretend it has proved it. My beliefs I test on my body, on my intuitional consciousness, and when I get a response there, then I accept." By now I know that when I'm not supposed to do something I immediately feel uneasiness, or "dis-ease," that can sometimes border on the feeling of foreboding, depending on the situation. Likewise, when the message is one of comfort, it's a good indication that it is probably best to proceed. If I heed those messages and follow those leads, everything turns out OK. But if I choose to ignore those messages and start rationalizing and twisting the truth until reality becomes unrecognizable, I suffer unnecessary and often unpleasant consequences. Following a path of denial leads to self-doubt, which sets in motion a chain of events that brings about a complex of complications and problems. We end up sending out the wrong messages and people react to them, which causes more confusion. Misunderstandings multiply and the situation begins to spiral out of control to the point where the chance of recovery gets farther and farther away from us. Once self-doubt sets in, we run the risk of losing ourselves entirely, losing our sense of reality. We then make decisions that have no basis in truth and such decisions invariably lead us down the wrong road.

As a result of suffering the consequences of negating my initial "gut" feelings, I now try to be much more aware of what my first reaction is to a given situation, and to follow it before I start the process of either rationalizing it away or allowing myself to be manipulated by someone else into making decisions that I know deep in my soul are not right for me. I can certainly relate to the words of Ralph Waldo Emerson: "All the mistakes I make arise from forsaking my own station and trying to see the object from another person's point of view." I don't need to "walk in someone else's shoes" to know the truth of a matter when my intuitive intelligence is telling me very clearly everything I need to know. The direction in which I should proceed is easy to recognize because my "gut" is always correct. Yet trying to see that correct decision through, and uphold it against a lifetime of conditioned responses and issues of codependency, can be a monumental challenge. The choice is ours, though, as to which path we follow and we ultimately bear the responsibility for those choices and the results they bring.

English writer G.K. Chesterton wrote, "I owe my success to having listened respectfully to the very best advice, and then going away and doing the exact opposite." Although it may seem like strange advice, I have done this on occasion when my intuition lead me that way, and it worked beautifully, particularly when I was writing theme songs for a film company that created some of the most iconic cartoon series in the history of television. The head of the music department became such a good friend to me and was so helpful to my having many successes in television. We first started working together when he was an executive at Columbia Pictures. One day he was honest enough to tell me that every time he gave me tips and directions about what the producers were looking for in a new television show's theme song, it was a good thing that I didn't follow his directions and went ahead and did exactly the opposite of what he had recommended. My high success rate proved that I did the right thing by following my own instincts. If we are going to be judged, it's better to be judged for what we believe in and not what we think someone else wants us to be or do.

Highly creative people seem to have a greater sensitivity to their inner voice and tend to embrace, rather than deny it, at least on the creative level. In an article in *The Journal of Creative Behavior* titled "Accessing the Further Reaches of Creative Potential," authors E. Paul Torrance and Laura K. Hall state: "Many of our great creative minds such as Mozart and Einstein have spoken of certain experiences which seem to transcend the deliberateness of the rational creative process. These experiences are often referred to as moments of 'insight, intuition, revelation' and are commonly described as occurring in an instant, creating a feeling of wholeness, a oneness 'with everything.'"[57]

Our intuition is our inner compass, our natural guidance system that we must depend upon to accurately direct every step on life's path. It is the light that illuminates our ability to make the right decisions with confidence and discernment at all times and in every situation. Just as a pilot depends on instruments when flying in low visibility, we too must depend on our intuition to safely guide us out of harm's way. Our intuition must be given first consideration in our quest to live a creative life. We must trust our creative intelligence and allow ourselves to express our truth without fear of judgment, steering clear of second-guessing ourselves, closing the channel of our creativity with "what if's." I am certainly no stranger to the challenges that unhealthy doubt presents, and two particular incidents stand out as good examples of this.

I was living in Singapore at the time I was writing the third movement of *Gates of Gold*, "Call of the Mountain." I got very excited about a particular section I was working on when suddenly a kind of dread feeling came over me. The ugly thought crept in that music critics and those of academia were going to clobber me with criticism for what I was writing. I stopped for a moment, took a deep breath, and decided that I was going to proceed with my initial feeling of joy and comfort instead of changing what I had written out of fear of what others would think. I did not want the fear of potential criticism to influence what I knew to be my truth. It turned out to be a good decision. "Call of the Mountain" has turned out to be one of the most requested and most performed compositions I have written.

The other example was while composing "Wind River (I Am)," commissioned by the University of Wyoming in celebration of the New Millennium. Toward the end of the piece, a very lush, melodic section had effortlessly unfolded, which really sang to my heart. But since the turn of the century, beautiful melodies in "modern" concert music seem to have become abhorrent to the intelligentsia of the art world, which made me cringe once again at the thought of the critical backlash I might receive.[58] So, I just sighed deeply and decided to go to sleep and leave the decision for the next day. Immediately upon awakening the next morning I played the melodic section again, and was so moved by its beauty, I emphatically said to myself, *This is staying!!!* I cannot accurately explain the great joy I felt when the conductor, who had no previous knowledge of my reservations about that melodic section, later said to me that to him, that lush section was the soul of the composition. Bingo!

Go with your "gut!" It won't let you down.

"Intuition is the essence of creativity."

Ingmar Bergman
Swedish producer and director

Intuition Quotations

Intuition Quotations

"Trust your hunches. They're usually based on facts filed away just below the conscious level."

Dr. Joyce Brothers
American psychologist, TV-radio personality, and author

"A hunch is creativity trying to tell you something."

Frank Capra
American film director

"It is the heart always that sees, before the head can see."

Thomas Carlyle
Scottish essayist, historian, and philosopher

"All great men are gifted with intuition. They know without reasoning or analysis, what they need to know."

Alexis Carrel
Nobel Prize winner in medicine and physiology

"The only real valuable thing is intuition."

Albert Einstein
German-born American physicist

"A moment's insight is sometimes worth a life's experience."

Oliver Wendell Holmes
American poet, essayist, and physician

"The power of intuitive understanding will protect you from harm until the end of your days."

Lao Tzu
Chinese philosopher and founder of Taoism

"I never know when I sit down, just what I am going to write. I make no plan; it just comes, and I don't know where it comes from."

D.H. Lawrence
English novelist, poet, and painter

"Intuitive insights, ESP, and epiphanies, I knew, are just different means for perceiving information."

Dr. Edgar Mitchell
Apollo 14 Astronaut, moonwalker, philosopher, and author

Creativity and Truth

Chapter Nine
Creativity and Truth

"Mysticism and creativity have this in common:
they require a person to live truthfully at every level of being."
Marilyn Whiteside
American author

Of all the wonderful qualities a person can possess, I find truthfulness to be most important to me, because it shows respect, caring and honor not only to others but also to ourselves. It allows us the courtesy of being able to make choices based on accurate knowledge, which helps us to make better decisions and better choices in any given context or situation. Truthfulness shows the sincere willingness to find a solid starting point from which we can create harmony and unity both microcosmically and macrocosmically.

We know truth because it is written in our hearts. It is the foundation of all that is, and despite the seemingly endless attempts to destroy it, it is indestructible. We know truth through intuitive insights. Truth embodies the spectrum of love. It is the first step on the road that leads to wisdom and understanding, and is the fountain from which all life, all creation springs forth. Truthfulness is the unequivocal benchmark of a person's character, in quality, integrity and scope, from which trusting relationships can be built, whether it be trusting ourselves, trusting our relationship to others, or trusting our relationship with the source of our creativity. Truth is the voice of our creative spirit and the infallible guide that illumines our way and points us in the right direction. Truth is its own goal.

> "Truth is. Belief not required."
>
>   Gerry Roston

Some of the definitions I have found of "truth" are:

· "A fact that has been verified."[59]
· "Something that corresponds to fact or reality."[60]
· "Honesty, sincerity, or integrity."[61]
· "Fidelity to an original or standard."[62]
· "Sincerity in action, character, and utterance."[63]

But the ones that speak most clearly to my soul are the following:

· "A transcendent fundamental or spiritual reality."[64]
· "That which is considered to be the supreme reality and to have the ultimate meaning and value of existence."[65]
· "The quality of being true."[66]

Since everything in the universe is interconnected, honesty has a great impact on the quality and outcome of our work. Successful businesswoman Mary Kay Ash, the founder of Mary Kay Cosmetics, believes that, "Honesty is the cornerstone of all success, without which confidence and ability to perform shall cease to exist." The same is true of our creative expression; its beauty and power are also greatly affected by our truthfulness in a number of ways. First of all, if we are not honest with ourselves, we will not be able to reflect who we really are in our creative works, getting stuck in an endless loop of imitation, floundering in a sea of self-doubt, allowing ourselves to be buffeted around by the opinions of others. As the singer and actress Pearl Bailey so simply stated, "You never find yourself until you face the truth." Secondly, our thoughts and intentions are vibration, and those vibrations become translated into our creative expression. If we are not honest, that will be reflected in our works. They will not be believable. Music is vibration, so it will show up there. Color is vibration, so it will appear in the colors that an artist chooses. *Everything* is vibration so it will show up in all that we do.

We are what we create. The fruits of our creativity are a reflection of who we are, and like an apple that looks great on the outside but is rotten on the inside, we cannot disguise the truth of ourselves or our work with fast talk and a false front for very long. Once past the thin outer skin, the truth will be revealed. The truth will *always* be revealed. We communicate the truth of who we are on a very deep level. We communicate through pheromones, the communicator molecules that deal with the raw data of who and what we are, and not the phony, fear-based façade that most people seem to hide behind.[67] Beauty of any kind is based in truth, and "Truth is the secret of eloquence and of virtue, the basis of moral authority; it is the highest summit of art and of life." Those poetic words of Swiss philosopher Frederic Amiel are themselves an expression of truth, as are the words of English writer G.K. Chesterton, who wrote, "The first and last thing required of genius is the love of truth."

Although the truth can sometimes feel very painful and hard to face, it is a law that stands unshakeable. No matter how much the truth hurts at times, it remains the cornerstone of our being, and it is only through truth that we can fully learn the lessons that we are here to learn. Without learning these lessons with dignity, honesty and humility, we end up just a shadow of our true selves, just empty shells of what we could've been had we had the courage to live a life based in truth. Life then, would've been just a masquerade and consequently a waste.

We must not be afraid to question ourselves, question *everything* in pursuit of truth, and must be willing to accept the answers we find and apply them accordingly in our lives. Truth will help to insure our safe passage as we travel our designated paths along life's journey, and living truthfully will help us to evolve to higher levels of awareness. Once our lives are firmly rooted in truth, we can move forward with confidence and ease, safe in knowing that the wisdom and discernment we have cultivated as a result of living truthfully, will help to insure our ultimate happiness, good health and success.

"We know the truth, not only by the reason, but also by the heart."

Blaise Pascal
French mathematician, philosopher, and physicist

Truth Quotations

Truth Quotations

"A liar will not be believed, even when he speaks the truth."

Aesop
Greek writer

"I love you, and because I love you, I would sooner have you hate me for telling you the truth than adore me for telling you lies."

Pietro Aretino
Italian poet, writer, and dramatist

"Where is there dignity unless there is honesty?"

Marcus Tullius Cicero
Roman orator, statesman, philosopher, and writer

"Lying to ourselves is more deeply ingrained than lying to others."

Feodor Dostoevsky
Russian writer, founder of existentialism

"The ideas that have lighted my way have been kindness, beauty and truth."

Albert Einstein
German-born American physicist

"Honesty, it seems, is supported by our biochemicals, and it only slows us down to choose otherwise."

Dr. Candace Pert
American neuroscientist and author

"No legacy is so rich as honesty."

William Shakespeare
English dramatist and poet

"Between whom there is hearty truth, there is love."

Henry David Thoreau
American philosopher and naturalist

"Kindness and honesty can only be expected from the strong."

Unknown Author

Creativity and Right Living

Chapter Ten
Creativity and Right Living

*"The most important human endeavor is
the striving for morality in our actions.
Our inner balance, and even our very existence depends on it.
Only morality in our actions
can give beauty and dignity to our lives."*
Albert Einstein
German-born American physicist

For me, right living has the greatest impact on keeping the channel open for the flow of creativity as applies to love and creating loving results. When I'm living honestly and feeling very "centered" spiritually, that flow seems endless and effortless. However, when I'm feeling out of balance, or unintentionally stray from a path of right living, the channel seems to close. I know the bliss of having that channel open so I make sure that I'm living a life that will insure that channel staying open. But what is "right living?" Although some aspects may vary from person to person, I believe the basics of right living are a very consistent part of a universal law. They include honesty, kindness, caring, compassion, purity of body, mind, and spirit, decency, modesty, generosity, empathy, unselfishness, understanding, and above all, love, just to name a few.

But how do we maintain right living in a world where good values and personal integrity have become nearly extinct, a world where people have become so desensitized that they no longer know what love is and therefore cannot express it even in the simplest ways? How do we maintain right living in a world where many people no longer have decency, self-respect or respect for others? The results of this demoralization of right living have created a seeming epidemic of mental, emotional and physical illness, and a profoundly deep sense of loneliness and isolation that are crippling, despite the number of "friends" one has or despite the voluminous number of sexual partners one has had. Sexuality, in its most sacred and supreme form, is a bridge that takes us to higher levels of consciousness.[68] Instead, the ultimate beauty of intimacy has been reduced to sport and recreation, leaving most who follow that destructive dead-end path unable to either be *truly* intimate or recognize it at all. It's a depressing reality that is leading to the same place it has not only lead individual people throughout history, but also most of the great civilizations: into ruin.

So, in order to attempt right living it's important to make sure that everything we take in, from the food we eat to the music we listen to, from the books and magazines we read to the movies and TV we watch, to the company we keep, are all uplifting in some way and contribute to the purity of our body, mind, and spirit. That's not an easy thing to do in the world we live in. Everything has become quite tainted. The food we eat has all the life processed out of it, has been genetically altered into something other than what nature intended, or has been bombarded with harmful chemicals in the name of profits. Our water, the very gift that comprises seventy percent of our body, is generally polluted. So much of the various forms of entertainment have likewise become devoid of goodness and love, with more emphasis being placed on "shock value" rather than content, whether it is sex or violence, or both. The entertainment industry seems to have no conscience and willfully caters to the lowest common denominator in order to increase profits and meet or exceed shareholders' expectations.

Concerning our very personal life and who we "bond" with, we must make sure that we are aligned with those whose energy and spirit are "positive," healthy, *truly* loving, and helpful to our spiritual, emotional, and creative growth in the very best ways. Although it would seem logical that everyone has some amount of goodness in them, it certainly appears that most don't choose to live anywhere near their full potential in this way; rather, *choosing* to behave in very hurtful and destructive ways, not only to others but ultimately to themselves. We cannot hurt others without ultimately hurting ourselves. We must also be very careful who we "bond" with intimately because as the wisdom of many of the greatest spiritual teachings warn, we take on the negative energy and "garbage" of those whose lives are misaligned, and the more intimate the connection, the greater the risk of being adversely affected, and the effects are very insidious.[69]

We have to examine why everything has become so tainted. The intentions behind all of the above are motivated by a conscious agenda of greed, manipulation, and selfishness, which are all forms of fear, and fear is the killer of true creativity. How we live our lives affects every aspect of everything we do. Unfortunately the masses seem to easily fall prey to fear's negative power and as a result, the collective consciousness of our societies has become very compromised. The "norm" has become quite warped, where "good" has become "bad" and "right" has become "wrong," and where "light" has become "darkness."

The truth has become twisted beyond recognition to the point that the whole world seems to be spinning out of control, lacking focus or center. Anyone outside the circle of the current trends is considered "square," "un-hip," and generally out of fashion. But in the end, fashions and trends pass and often leave a very bitter aftertaste. In Irish playwright Oscar Wilde's own words of wisdom: "Fashion is a form of ugliness so intolerable that we have to alter it every six months." The issue of the masses going off to the slaughter has much to do with people surprisingly preferring to be told and *sold* what to do rather than deciding for themselves. That action is one of the enemies of right living and living in a creatively truthful way. As the saying goes, "If you don't think for yourself, someone else will do it for you." This is not an expression of a life rooted in love and creativity.

I have come to experience the universe as being very impersonal. It doesn't matter who you are, what you look like, where you live, what race you are, where you come from, how much money you have, how many good deeds you have done, or anything else. If you violate the universal laws in force, there are consequences. It's not about reward or punishment. It's about there being a universal reaction to our actions, and no amount of rationalization lessens the force of the universe's response, for better or for worse. It's basically simple math: "we reap what we sow" and that's that. Fashion, trends, or rationalization have no power and have no meaning. However, we cannot take the reaction of the universe, whether favorable or unfavorable, personally. It's just what it is. However impersonal, though, the adverse effects on us, as well as others, can still be devastating and very long lasting.

Everything we do has an effect on us psychologically and physiologically. Wrong action wears down a person mentally and I think that's evident by the epidemic of mental illness in our world. The wisdom of German philosopher Goethe's words are truer than ever: "We do not have to visit a madhouse to find disordered minds; our planet is the mental institution of the universe." Wrong action also takes its toll on people physically through various diseases and conditions and creates the general lack of well-being that is plaguing our societies, sending people en-mass to doctors, therapists, specialists, and in search of alternative methods of healing. The price paid is reflected in a great loss of time, energy, and money, with few favorable and lasting results. That's because the problem is on a very deep level and cannot be eradicated with "magic bullets," prescriptions, or other hopeful, but short-lived and ineffective quick fixes. Wrong living wears a person down to the breaking point in one form or another. On the other hand, the good we do also has a reaction from the universe, although many people feel their good deeds go un-rewarded, and believe that some people get away with murder, literally and metaphorically. But I don't believe that, in the larger scheme of things. No one gets away with *anything*. And likewise, our good works do not go unrewarded. The question we must ask ourselves though is: "what is it that we are seeking as a reward?" If the good deeds we have done, and good works we continue to do have their basis in love, then the joy derived from the goodness we create and unselfishly share, is the reward itself. Anything up and above that I consider "icing on the cake."

How we live our lives while we are here has a tremendous effect on the quality and power of our creative expression, what form it takes, and ultimately what kind of impact it will have on others. Will the results be far-reaching and long lasting in positive or negative ways? Will they damage, heal, or ultimately be of little consequence, be forgotten and have relatively no effect at all? Dr. Masaru Emoto, the author of *The Hidden Messages in Water* reveals, "Just as a drop in a pond creates a ripple that spreads out endlessly, the deformity of even one soul spreads throughout the world, resulting in global deformities. But all is not lost . . . there is hope. There is salvation, and it's called 'love and gratitude.'"[70]

Right living keeps the channel open to receive the bountiful flow of love, creativity, and goodness beyond what we might have ever imagined. Since we are electro-magnetic energy, the shift in our consciousness to right living creates a kind of magnetism that attracts to us all that we need and more. People gravitate toward us in loving ways; they seem to identify with the goodness we radiate. Opportunities appear that allow us to live our truth and fulfill our dreams. All the resources we need to live a loving, creative life materialize. We then have the joyful opportunity to share our prosperity, good fortune, and creative bounty with others in a variety of ways, helping them too to find their own way on the path of right living, the path that leads to creative fulfillment.

> "When you were born, you cried and the world rejoiced. Live your life so that when you die, the world cries and you rejoice."
>
> Cherokee Expression

Right Living Quotations

Right Living Quotations

"Moral excellence comes about as a result of habit. We become just by doing just acts, temperate by doing temperate acts, brave by doing brave acts."

Aristotle
Greek philosopher

"The best things in life aren't things."

Art Buchwald
American journalist, author, and screenwriter

"The greatest use of life is to spend it for something that will outlast it."

William James
American philosopher and psychologist

"I am for those means which will give the greatest good to the greatest number."

Abraham Lincoln
Sixteenth President of the United States

"I have held many things in my hands, and I have lost all of them, but whatever I have placed in God's hands, that I still possess."

Martin Luther
German reformation leader

"The time you enjoy wasting is not wasted time."

Bertrand Russell
Mathematician and philosopher

"You cannot be happy when the rest of the mankind is unhappy. Share your prosperity with others; strive to alleviate the suffering of others. That is your duty."

Sai Baba
Indian spiritual teacher

"There is no right way to do a wrong thing."

Unknown author

"Associate with men of good quality if you esteem your own reputation; for it is better to be alone than in bad company."

George Washington
First President of the United States

Creativity and Self-Esteem

Chapter Eleven
Creativity and Self-Esteem

"No one can make you feel inferior without your consent."
Eleanor Roosevelt
American social activist and stateswoman

I think it's sad and very unfortunate that so many people greatly confuse "ego" for "self-esteem." It's dangerous because this misunderstanding is at the root of so much misery and confusion. I have heard the following statement parroted over and over again by so many over the years: "In order to do anything well you must have a healthy ego." I believe that statement is *absolutely false!* We don't need a healthy *ego* to do well, we need good *self-esteem* to do well, and there is a tremendous difference between the two. There is a *chasm* of difference between the two.

According to Eastern philosophy, we must actually *destroy* our ego because it is one of the biggest obstacles to the spiritual growth that leads to enlightenment and liberation. It is an opaque veil between us and self-realization, self-knowingness. Ego is an exaggerated sense of self-importance having no basis in truth. It fools us into believing that we are greatly superior to others. This whole ego-related delusion about "I'm better than you," "I'm stronger than you," "I'm more successful than you," is so *terribly* unevolved. It's *so boring.* There are countless examples of people I have encountered in the entertainment world alone whose *huge* displays of ego were very obvious covers for their gross insecurity and low self-esteem. That certainly doesn't seem very "healthy" to me. The ego is a big fraud. On the other hand, self-esteem is the understanding and appreciation of our *true* value and worth based on *accurate knowledge*. It is the gauge, the readout that lets us know how and what we feel about ourselves. It also indicates the quality and level of respect we have for ourselves. Unlike ego, it is *not* an inflated sense of self-worth, stuck in the primordial muck of primitive posturing. Healthy self-esteem in based in truth.

To allow healthy self-esteem to unfold naturally, we need to rid ourselves of our shortcomings, and we can only do that by first acknowledging them, *without* condemnation, and preferably with loving concern. Of equal importance, we must also acknowledge our strengths and our noble qualities, and that too must be based on accurate knowledge. That's why right living is so important. If we stay out of nature's way and allow it, good self-esteem will arise naturally from living truthfully and honorably. Once again, it's more physics than a product of personal will. The fruits of our deeds determine how we will ultimately feel about ourselves. Both good self-esteem and low self-esteem are a logical consequence of the way we choose to live our lives, although low self-esteem, at times, can be the product of a distorted self-image that, like the ego, is not based in truth.

There can be many unfortunate reasons for low self-esteem, but let's hope that if in fact we are *not* living honorably, and *not* honoring our creative truth, that we will feel enough discomfort to be more than motivated to make the necessary changes in our lives that will insure we attain the state of personal and emotional health and well-being that allows us to flourish creatively. We need to listen to our discomforts and not discount the "dis-ease" we feel, but instead acknowledge it and ask, "Why is this bothering me, what does it mean, and what should I do about it?" The real answers are usually very clear if we are completely honest with ourselves. From there, the next issue is whether we want to accept the responsibilities that come along with those answers and then take the required action.

Pain and discomfort serve a noble purpose in our lives and although they can sometimes feel unbearable and are something we would prefer to do without, they do serve to protect us. Personally, I would not trade sensitivity for insensitivity because that renders creativity lifeless and empty, without color, without beauty, devoid of meaning. In order for us to evolve creatively we must allow ourselves to truly "feel" and find our guidance from what those feelings, including the pain and discomfort, are telling us. Denying those discomforts is like trying to bury our dirty laundry. But denying it won't make it go away. It will still be there and will get nastier the longer we fail to attend to it. And although some of our past deeds may be things we wish to forget, if we acknowledge them truthfully, make amends when and where we can, and turn our lives around, we can *then* look at our errors and consider them as important steps in our growth. But do not be misled: they are *not* important steps in our growth until we face them honestly, *admit* to ourselves, to others, and to our Higher Power, the truth of our wrongdoings, learning from them and not repeating them. As usual, we have a choice.

Too many people, lost in the swirling deluded fog of New Age double talk, refuse to accept accountability for their actions by hiding behind the false notion that *everything* is valuable, OK, and just perfect. Well, everything *is not* OK! If everything *were* OK, then there would be no need for laws, but unfortunately, our species has not evolved to that point yet. We must avoid hiding behind the self-defeating fallacy that anything we do is OK because we are just "perfect as we are" at any given point in time. (Well, isn't that convenient!?) So then, if one is to hide behind that blind of untruth, then one must also forgive all those responsible throughout history for all the misery and suffering they caused countless *millions* of people, because just *maybe*, they were doing the best they could too. Maybe they were having a "bad day." If we are going to make excuses for ourselves we must also make the same allowances for everybody else, *without exception!* I believe as the philosopher Goethe, "Treat people as if they were what they ought to be and you help them to become what they are capable of being." The point here is that we *all* must take responsibility for the things we do, the things we say, and even the things we *think*. Every action has a reaction and it would serve us well to create a karmic account whose dividends include the creation and sustenance of healthy self-esteem.

"Too many people overvalue what they are not and undervalue what they are."

Malcolm Forbes
American publisher

Self-Esteem Quotations

Self-Esteem Quotations

"Instead of thinking about what you're missing, try thinking about what you have that everyone else is missing."

Anonymous

"Why compare yourself with others? No one in the entire world can do a better job of being you than you."

Anonymous

"Feelings of inferiority and superiority are the same. They both come from fear."

Dr. Robert Anthony
American management educator and writer

"A person's worth in this world is estimated according to the value they put on themselves."

Jean de la Bruyere
French philosopher

"You yourself, as much as anybody in the entire universe, deserve your love and affection."

Buddha
Hindu Prince Siddhartha Gautama, founder of Buddhism

"Nothing builds self-esteem and self-confidence like accomplishment."

Thomas Carlyle
Scottish essayist, historian, and philosopher

"Your chances of success in any undertaking can always be measured by your belief in yourself."

Robert Collier
American motivational author

"Low self-esteem is like driving through life with your hand-brake on."

Maxwell Maltz
American author

"It is a funny thing about life: if you refuse to accept anything but the best—you very often get it."

W. Somerset Maugham
American author

Creativity and Commitment

Chapter Twelve
Creativity and Commitment

"The quality of a man's life is in direct proportion
to his commitment to excellence,
regardless of his chosen field of endeavor."

Vince Lombardi
American football coach

Anything we choose to do in life requires commitment to be able to do it with excellence. However when you love so powerfully, commitment arises naturally without thought or effort. It is effortless and without question because love and commitment are synonymous. There is no *true* love without commitment and without it none of the sweet fruits of love blossom. Johann Wolfgang von Goethe's insight was so clear and accurate when he stated:

> "Until one is committed, there is hesitancy, the chance to draw back, always ineffectiveness. Concerning all acts of initiative and creation, there is one elementary truth the ignorance of which kills countless ideas and splendid plans: that the moment one definitely commits oneself, then providence moves too. All sorts of things occur to help one that would never otherwise have occurred. A whole stream of events issues from the

decision, raising in one's favor all manner of unforeseen incidents, meetings and material assistance which no man could have dreamed would have come his way. Whatever you can do or dream you can, begin it. Boldness has genius, power and magic in it. Begin it now."

Commitment gives us the strength and courage to stay on the path that leads to what it is we love. And the resulting passion and enthusiasm for the focus of our love helps us to endure and get past all the obstacles we may encounter along the way. Commitment's role in success is basically part of a very simple equation.

In any relationship, there must be commitment whether it is a relationship involving people, our relationship with our creative wishes, or our relationship with ourselves. Commitment is a pledge of devotion and dedication. It's a promise to give everything we have to someone or something we love, without question. But we must make sure that the focus of our commitment is worthy of such unbending devotion and unquestioning dedication to begin with, or else our honest efforts are just a futile waste of time, energy, and love. And in any relationship, the commitment must be mutual or failure is pretty much guaranteed. Those who won't commit usually fail to do so out of fear, and it should be clear by now that fear and love are not synonymous. We must see through our unfounded fears and honestly consider our *healthy* concerns of commitment, keeping in mind psychologist Rollo May's words: "Commitment is healthiest when it is not without doubt but in spite of doubt."[71] When the commitment is between the universe and ourselves, we can be sure that the universe is committing. It very much reinforces the spiritual thought, *if you reach out your hand to me I will reach out my hand to you. If you take one step toward me I'll take two steps toward you.* We must initiate the process and take the first step in order to set the universe in motion and materialize whatever it is that we hope for. And there must be a mutual agreement, solidarity of purpose, direction, and intent, based in truth.

When we truly love and make a firm commitment to see our creative or personal vision through, we then set the wheels of the universe in motion to see it through to its fulfillment.

"Wheresoever you go, go with all your heart."
Confucius
Chinese philosopher

Commitment Quotations

Commitment Quotations

"Follow your bliss. Find where it is and don't be afraid to follow it."

Joseph Campbell
American author and mythologist

"Once you make a decision, the universe conspires to make it happen."

Ralph Waldo Emerson
American philosopher, essayist, and lecturer

"Your word is your promise, so when you say something you must have the determination to commit yourself."[72]

Masaru Emoto
Japanese author and doctor of alternative medicine

"Promises are like the full moon, if they are not kept at once they diminish day by day."

German Proverb

"Life is like a parking garage: if you go backward, you get severe tire damage."

Ivan Hoffman
American author

"Something in human nature causes us to start slacking off at our moment of greatest accomplishment. As you become successful, you will need a great deal of self-discipline not to lose your sense of balance, humility and commitment."

H. Ross Perot
American businessman

"I believe life is constantly testing us for our level of commitment, and life's greatest rewards are reserved for those who demonstrate a never-ending commitment to act until they achieve. This level of resolve can move mountains, but it must be constant and consistent. As simplistic as this may sound, it is still the common denominator separating those who live their dreams from those who live in regret."

Anthony Robbins
American motivational speaker and writer

"The true creator is both willing and able to make a commitment, to immerse her/himself in a problem to the point that it virtually becomes an obsession, overriding all other interests."

Marilyn Whiteside
American author

Creativity and Overcoming Obstacles

Chapter Thirteen
Creativity and Overcoming Obstacles

"Life shrinks or expands in proportion to one's courage."

Anais Nin

French-American writer

I must confess that there are times I feel afraid of the unknown, regarding the day-to-day raw survival as an artist striving in what sometimes feels like a harsh and unsupportive creative environment. But then I feel excited about what I can learn from the challenges I may face, what hidden beauty the challenges may bring out in me, and where those challenges may lead me as I explore the uncharted territory of myself traveling through the field of infinite possibilities. Overcoming obstacles seems to be a constant, but trying to overcome them with dignity and honor seems to create a very powerful beauty in us, an omnipresent radiance that beams forth, touching, inspiring, and transforming all in its path. Its reach is infinite, permeating every corner of Divine consciousness and carrying the collective mind and soul along with it. Author Marilyn Whiteside, in *The Journal of Creative Behavior*, expressed so poetically, "Creators are courageous. They are able to accept the polarities in their nature, and they are willing to make sacrifices in defense of their convictions. They have a sense of destiny, a sense of having been chosen to reveal some facet of the life source. This same courage aids them in scaling the barriers between conscious and unconscious thinking; it enables them to risk madness and a loss of personal identity in pursuit of an ultimate truth . . . Bravery on the Battlefield is sometimes great, and bravery in the endurance of the commonplace and the petty is frequently even greater; but the ultimate courage is in the willingness to see—really see—one's self and, in that self, the face of one's Creator."[73]

I am certainly no stranger to taking risks, that's for sure. Coming to Hollywood at 25 years old without hardly knowing anyone was a huge leap of faith, especially since I "cold turkeyed," moving from Japan with little money, basically no support, and one of the most competitive and crowded industries in the world in front of me. The main things in my favor were my dreams, my passion and love for music, and a lifetime of hard work that prepared me to meet the huge challenge ahead with courage, one-pointedness, and a very loving spirit. As Navajo code talker Peter MacDonald stated: "We must dare to dream great dreams . . . and then we must dare to put them into action." I must admit there were times I felt very frightened . . . *very* frightened, very alone, and very vulnerable. But knowing that I had not only to survive, but to flourish, *because I had to*, gave me a kind of "supernatural" strength to face all the challenges that lay ahead of me both professionally and personally in pursuit of living my truth, my "dharma," my purpose in life. The following words of billionaire H. Ross Perot, really sum it up: "We have to succeed, so we will."

I don't know where the time went, but I have been able to experience so many amazing things that are beyond what I had imagined at the start of this journey. And the really interesting thing is that I feel the best is still to come. Looking back, I can see how previously unimaginable dreams materialized out of nothing more than *thoughts* that had an unbending follow-through. Little by little those good thoughts and a pure heart brought all the right people and circumstances into my life that would help me to see so many of those dreams through to fruition. Even with very little money, and in the early days, no idea of where work was going to come from, every sunny day still gave me hope because at least I was among greatness, immersed in the rich creative talent pool of Los Angeles. These were people with dreams too, who came to the big "dream machine" to materialize the wishes of their hearts, souls, and minds. Even as I struggled to make my own way, I felt very touched by the courage and love of so many people who were striving to realize their dreams too.

I felt an especially soft spot in my heart for those who came with families, having the added responsibilities of insuring their safety, comfort, and happiness, trying to juggle it all and make things work. Yet in a way, they were fortunate to have one another for love, support and grounding, which is a very valuable treasure and asset. The wisdom of this is verified in the words of the Chinese philosopher Lao Tzu: "Being deeply loved by someone gives you strength, while loving someone deeply gives you courage." That kind of loving family support was something I unfortunately didn't have at the time and had to make do without. The weight of that reality was sometimes oppressive, but on the flip side it gave me a lot of freedom and flexibility to keep on my path without having to subject anyone else to the challenges and obstacles that presented themselves all along the way, and there were certainly many. However, I don't think there is a better or best way. It has more to do with what our needs are, what we feel comfortable with, and also what we have to accept about the circumstances and conditions of our lives at the time. Whatever the circumstances are, where there is a will there is way.

Soon I would be blessed with a family of new friends, who like me were giving everything they had to give in pursuit of realizing their creative vision, and doing it with such love, which to me is the very important key. We encouraged one another to keep going when we felt discouraged, and consoled one another during the struggles and seemingly endless amount of rejections we all faced and *still* face from time to time. But, we also celebrated our thrilling and surreal successes together, which were certainly sweeter because of all we had sacrificed and endured to get there. We were happy for each other's success, and as we climbed our own ladders of accomplishment we helped pull one another up and shared our new level of creative reality when we were able. At the very least, we served as an inspiration to one another, knowing well where we had come from. We could see the tangible evidence that dreams *do* come true, and that somehow we were all very important parts of each other's triumphs. I still believe that "success," whatever that means to a person, is a group effort. We don't really do anything alone. We need others. We need others to believe in us and we need others with the "keys to the kingdom" to open the doors that lead to fulfilling our life's purpose. And hopefully there comes a time when we too hold the keys that can help unlock the doors of opportunity for others.

The issue of "location" often comes up when people speak of their struggles pursuing a creative life, often complaining about the lack of opportunities where they live. I did move across the country, via Japan, to pursue my dreams, but not everyone needs to uproot in order to live their creative truth. Moving is one option, but *not* the only one. We can create opportunities *no matter where we are*. Something very important to consider, though, is how the quality of our lives will be affected by where we choose to live. Do we want to trade clean air and clean food, a sense of community connectedness, and the tranquil beauty of nature for pollution, crime, noise, and disintegration? A wise scripture recommends that we "calculate the cost."[74] To what degree are we willing to sacrifice the quality of our lives in pursuit of our dreams? And is there a way to find the best of both worlds? Sometimes there is a tradeoff involved and a comfortable balance can be attained. Who's to say what is right or wrong? These are very personal issues, and each of us has to search our own souls for the answers to these important questions. But whichever way we choose, simplifying our life helps to eliminate, or at least reduce the number of obstacles we might face, making the way clearer for us in our pursuit of creative fulfillment. In this light, and especially for those who have traveled a lot in search of their creative truth, the following words of Indian spiritual teacher Sai Baba, certainly ring true, "You cannot move freely when you are encumbered with burdens. Less luggage, more comfort, is the slogan for the journey of life,"[75] and that applies whether our creative pursuits involve traveling or not.

And then, sometimes we just have to *go for it!* Things may actually work out a lot easier than we imagined, with the quality of our lives becoming *better* than ever. Prepare the best you can, know the territory, but then go for the adventure with a positive, loving attitude and good intentions. Being steadfast in never compromising your personal and creative integrity in the process will help insure that no matter what the outcome, nothing can be lost, and at minimum, something valuable can be gained.

It is my understanding concerning infinity, that every point is the center of the universe, so wherever we are is as much the center of the universe both in location and in potential, as Hollywood, New York, London, or any place for that matter.[76] In the book *Black Elk Speaks*, Black Elk, the old medicine man, said that in his vision he saw himself on the central mountain of the world, Harney Peak, South Dakota. But he also said the central mountain of the world is *everywhere.*[77] This is in line with what sages of many cultures have been saying throughout time, including 12th Century texts that state, God is an intelligible sphere whose circumference is nowhere and center is everywhere.[78] I know the "pop" side of society says, *location* is everything, yet in reality the most valuable real estate is the fertile ground of one's imagination, and one's heart, where love resides and from which Divine beauty and powerful works can grow. The whole point is that we can create great works wherever we are. We need not look outside of ourselves for the source of creativity and success, but focus more within ourselves for the untapped well of creative riches.

In discussing overcoming obstacles, I must go back to a subject I addressed earlier: Truth. I believe that in order to truly overcome obstacles honorably, we must face our challenges with honesty, both with ourselves and with others. Honesty is a fundamental component to overcoming the obstacles that can hinder the kind of enduring success that has *real* meaning and lasting power. I'm inclined to say it takes courage to be honest, but being honest shouldn't be a courageous act at all. Actually it is a mindset, a reflex, a quality of the heart that develops over time with consistency of intent and action. Honesty should be a way of life and I highly recommend that anyone trying to overcome obstacles on their path of love and creativity make it their *only* way of facing challenges and dealing with relationships of any kind. Our moral integrity is the foundation and basis of all else that is good and worthwhile, and I believe it is the key to *real* success and true happiness in this life and beyond, and not the transient "pop" version of success and happiness that gets passed off as the real thing.

What can we do to overcome obstacles on our path of love and creativity? Well, for one thing, I pray a lot. I pray for guidance. I try to make my intentions clear but I also pray that whatever is best will come to be. I pray for the strength and discernment to face, and at least try to understand the answers to those prayers, especially if they're not the answers I had hoped for. One of my best friends says that, "Rejection is protection," and I know from experience that sometimes this is very true. We lose something only to find something better waiting for us at the next turn.

As I continue to learn not only from my own personal experiences, but also from the unfortunate experiences of others, I have found that it is crucial to know when to cut our losses and move on before the damage created by unhealthy relationships, circumstances, and desires, becomes irreparable. And this damage continues to reverberate on into the future, unfortunately affecting everything we do, and everyone and everything we come in contact with. This is where faith comes in; faith in ourselves, and faith in our Higher Power, that whatever we need will be provided to us, especially if our hearts and intentions are pure; faith that if we follow those good intentions through, we will have the strength and conviction to do what is best, what is right. The famous Serenity Prayer can help us:

"God, grant me the serenity to accept the things I cannot change, the courage to change the things I can, and the wisdom to know the difference."[79]

None of us are exempt from facing things we cannot change, and know how hard it can be to accept those things as they are. We all face these kinds of challenges in our lives no matter where we come from, what we do for a living, or how successful we may be. But we can minimize the number and severity of the challenges we face in life by using good judgment based on a strong moral foundation that is rooted in truth. That moral foundation might appear slightly different for different people but the underlying truth is the same and non-negotiable. It's a spiritual law that does not entertain or give way to rationalizations.

Another thing I do in trying to overcome obstacles is ask the help and guidance of people I trust, perhaps those who have gone through what I am going through and can see more clearly than I can due to their experience and garnered wisdom. Einstein said, "Problems cannot be solved at the same level of awareness that created them." Very often we are so clouded and overwhelmed by the close proximity to our troubles that we cannot see things clearly enough to resolve them. Once we understand and accept this, it is the beauty of our humility that allows us to unashamedly reach out to others for help, which is a sign, not of weakness, but an indication of great strength and courage. It's very valuable when others, who have an unclouded view, can help us have a better perspective of things. Even if that's not the case, then at least we can release to the universe whatever it is we have on our minds. Sometimes just verbalizing it, getting it out, helps us to get closer to finding our own solutions. Talking things out can help us to feel that a huge weight has been lifted off of us.

There are many books, both ancient and new, that are devoted to helping us overcome obstacles. The sacred books of many of the world's religions and spiritual philosophies offer great wisdom and guidance. We should keep an open mind to them, knowing that we don't have to buy the whole package if we don't want to. We can take what we need and leave the dogma behind. We can also read the inspiring biographies and autobiographies of people who have overcome their own challenges despite adversities, having gone on to do great things. Experiencing the wisdom of the mystic poets who had such remakable insight into the true nature of this world we live in can also help and inspire us to see a bigger picture. Reading such inspired works can help us to gain our own foresight concerning the true nature of life and where it leads. The Indian Vedas and ancient Buddhist writings, for example, discuss truths that only in recent times, science has suddenly claimed to have "discovered." I remember attending a lecture of a group of world-renowned physicists who were talking about the trip they had just made to visit the Dalai Lama. In their meeting with him they were excitedly telling him about a "new" discovery they had made in physics and his response was something to the effect, *You just found out?* This information is recorded in ancient Tibetan Buddhist texts that are thousands of years old!

Further, in the process of seeking help, some enjoy the fellowship of others, while some prefer to work things out themselves. I guess there is no right or wrong in this case, but I do keep in mind a lovely Swedish proverb: "Shared joy is a double joy; shared sorrow is half a sorrow." Whatever works best for each person would be the proper choice. It all depends on our individual needs and style, what we feel comfortable with. Then there is just being still . . . Quiet introspection may be the perfect non-action to take when we feel it to be best. Meditation has also proven to be very helpful to so many people in trying to not only find answers to their questions, but also for general well-being. When we are in good health we have more clarity and energy with which to overcome our challenges.

Lastly, we can just have fun! Sometimes temporarily letting go of the problems or challenges and just relaxing can free both our subconscious and unconscious minds into revealing the best ways to proceed. I remember one incident very well when I was experiencing what others might incorrectly call a "writer's block." After several years of hoping to someday write a work for orchestra, "Arrival: A View From Sea" from *Gates of Gold* unfolded so fast, in complete detail, without warning, seemingly out of nowhere! The flow of information was so intense and happening so fast I was wondering how I was going to keep up. Eight hours of composing seemed like two minutes. But then, around eight hours into this experience it was as if the creative faucet was suddenly turned off. I had reached a wall and could go no further. I had arrived at what would later become the mid-point of the piece and felt like I was on empty. The flow just stopped as unexpectedly as it had started and that was that. I was so excited about all the magic that had already unfolded that I wanted so badly to just keep it going, to stay in that magical place, but it seemed the well had gone dry.

The next morning I checked out what I had written the previous day and it was like discovering it for the first time! It was as if it had never taken place; as if it had all been a dream . . . I remember thinking to myself in complete amazement, *What is this???* Being understandably excited about this beautiful and magical creation, I wanted to keep working on it to its completion, but once again nothing unfolded, so I decided to go "play," to do something "fun" instead of banging my head against the cosmic wall. I drove to Los Angeles Union Station and spent several hours photographing trains and watching people come and go. I felt like a little kid, very free and unencumbered by life's problems and responsibilities. I guess it reminded me of the excitement and wonder of going to the train station when I was a child, totally thrilled about riding the train to New York City. Keeping our child-like spirit alive, no matter what age we may be, is very important in keeping the channel of creativity open. I know it's true for me.

As a result of letting go and having fun, the rest of the composition revealed itself on the return trip, while driving on the 101 freeway. I sped as fast as I could to get back as quickly as possible so I could actually notate the music I had heard playing in my soul. Great things happen when we let go of our attachment to the end results and just enjoy the ride, relaxing and having a bit of fun.

The following words of Marilyn Whiteside in *The Journal of Creative Behavior,* just verified and reinforced what I've already experienced:

> "The second stage in creative activity is less obviously related to the work at hand. It is a period of detached waiting, of incubation, when all conscious resources have been exhausted and no further progress seems possible. Accepting the apparent defeat, the creator takes a walk, goes fishing or naps. It is a time of calculated surrender: 'By letting go, it all gets done . . .' (Lao Tze)." Conscious thought, the weaker part of the psyche, now defers to the superior powers of the unconscious. Logic, judgment and will are temporarily relinquished in exchange for the buried data or for synthesis and clarification."[80]

We have to have our priorities straight before we can accomplish *anything* in life. We cannot put the cart before the horse. We must first and foremost live a life that is upright and honest, with the intent to help and heal, never to harm. We must try our best to live our lives by that simple Golden Rule: "Do unto others as we would like others to do unto us."[81] Just living by that simple rule could make this world transform into such a different experience than humankind has been having for the past thousands of years or more. We must have a solid foundation upon which to build our dreams; one that will withstand the weight of the challenges we may encounter; one that can withstand the winds of change and the storms we must weather.

Something I read in my early twenties, when I was just embarking on my professional creative path, has stayed with me throughout my life. It said that the difference between "successful" people and those who haven't succeeded was that successful people take note of problems as they arise but don't allow them stand in their way. They just keep going and keep it in mind to address the problems as they can.[82] I think it's important to keep a momentum going and not become derailed or sidetracked by challenges. Some obstacles we can remove immediately and some are just going to take a bit of time. But the most important thing is to just keep moving forward. Try to address the challenges as they arise, but above all, *keep going!*

If *anyone* has to believe in us, it is *us*. How can we expect others to believe in us if we don't even believe in ourselves? Once our own belief is firmly established it seems much easier to attract and materialize all that we need to fulfill our heart's desires. Although we cannot depend on others to do the believing for us, the more the merrier of course. All that positive energy and reinforcement helps.

It should be a great comfort and strength for us to know that we are not alone in our struggles to create beauty. We have the source of all creativity as our teacher and tower of strength, and that source resides in us. We are a reflection of that Supreme source, an extension of that infinite, inexhaustible Divine creative energy, so our success is insured if we allow ourselves to dare to be who we really are.

"When it is dark enough, you can see the stars."

Charles A Beard
American historian

Courage Quotations

Courage Quotations

"Courage and perseverance have a magical talisman, before which difficulties disappear and obstacles vanish into air."

John Quincy Adams
Sixth President of the United States

"I am not afraid of storms for I am learning how to sail my ship."

Louisa May Alcott
American novelist

"Most of the important things in the world have been accomplished by people who have kept on trying when there seemed to be no hope at all."

Dale Carnegie
American author

"To get through the hardest journey we need take only one step at a time, but we must keep on stepping."

Chinese proverb

"The important thing is this: To be able at any moment to sacrifice what we are for what we could become."

Charles DuBois
American artist

"Our greatest glory is not in never failing, but in rising up every time we fail."

Ralph Waldo Emerson
American philosopher, essayist, and lecturer

"Creativity requires the courage to let go of certainties."

Erich Fromm
American psychoanalyist and social philosopher

"Do what you can, with what you have, where you are."

Theodore Roosevelt
Twenty-sixth President of the United States

"Go confidently in the direction of your dreams. Live the life you have imagined."

Henry David Thoreau
American philosopher and naturalist

Creativity and Change

Chapter Fourteen
Creativity and Change

"You must be the change you wish to see in the world."

Mahatma Gandhi
Indian spiritual and political leader

Everything and everyone in the world as we know it, is in a constant state of change, transformation, evolution, creation, decay, and destruction. Even destruction brings about the creation of something new in both our circumstances and in our physical reality. I have come to learn that the only thing that doesn't change is change. We must be willing to let go of what we no longer need in order to allow what we *do* need to materialize. And we must do so without guilt. Author Marilyn Whiteside stated in *The Journal of Creative Behavior*, "Those who create must be willing and able to tear down existing ideas and structures (and even their own personalities) to make way for the new and untried. They must abandon tradition, with its certainties, in favor of innovation, with its uncertainties."[83]

Unhealthy attachment to things and ideas that no longer serve us well, if in fact they have *ever* served us well, can inhibit our forward movement and prevent us from evolving to our greatest potential. They prevent us from growing and having the wonderful new experiences we need that lead to the fulfillment of our wishes. As long as change is inevitable, we must go with the river's flow instead of fighting against the current, and strive to embrace the changes that are necessary for our betterment. We must accept change as an unavoidable part of this process we call living and to let it bring about the myriad colorful and interesting possibilities that await us and can offer to help accelerate our creative and personal growth.

It is important to avoid getting stuck in a loop of unhealthy patterns of living that put us in a position of repeating the same experiences again and again; choices that get us nowhere. But as strange as it may seem, there are those who prefer to repeat the same experiences, even to the detriment of their own growth, because those experiences are familiar to them and offer some kind of false security and comfort. To them, the "known," as bad as it may be, is more preferable and less frightening than the "unknown." But if we have to make a choice, it is better to be afraid of the known than to be afraid of the unknown, afraid of getting stuck in the monotony of the comfortably familiar that leads nowhere. Life is an adventure and we must welcome change, welcome the unknown with faith, hope, and child-like wonder, or be forced into changing against our will. One way or the other, change is going to take place whether we like it or not. The universe has its own perfect way of doing things and will bring about the changes that are necessary whether it suits our timetable or not. There is a saying: "If you don't create change, change will create you."[84] Remember that *healthy* changes are ultimately for our own good. Embrace them with a joyful spirit of love and gratitude.

> "There is nothing wrong with change, if it is in the right direction."
>
> Sir Winston Churchill

In order to initiate the changes we continually need to make in our lives, we must not only overcome fear, we must overcome guilt, which, if not based in truth, can be a heavy burden and a very huge obstacle to our growth. A healthy conscience is a great gift and asset to us. It is our divinely inspired guide that helps to direct our lives and keeps us from harming others as well as ourselves. However, in the wrong hands, guilt can be a very powerful weapon of control that both individuals and organizations with less than honorable motives, use *without* conscience. Some religions, in the words of philosopher Alan Watts, "have institutionalized guilt as a virtue."[85] They lead us to believe that it is something spiritually noble, something that will gain us merit. In this way, so many people wear their suffering as a badge of honor. Sacrificing one's self to guilt is *not* a noble endeavor as we are often led to believe.

I am neither a fan nor a follower of the martyrdom syndrome and most certainly do not believe in the "no pain no gain" philosophy either. Suffering is *not* a ticket to great rewards in heaven as many have chosen to believe. Although we can learn something valuable from even the most unpleasant or unfortunate experiences, why have such experiences if they are unnecessary? There are many different ways to learn the same lessons, many roads that lead to the same destination. The choice is ours, so why not make better choices to begin with? Human beings are fairly resilient, but the third-dimensional laws of nature are in force and when the bill is due for the debt we have accrued, you can depend on the Universe to be there right on time to collect what it's owed, very often *with interest.*

As mentioned earlier, pain can be a very effective motivator to initiate change in our lives. It exists as a barometer with which to gauge our experiences and gives us a clear indication that something is not right and must change. Why is it, then, that people seem to understand this more easily physically than emotionally? Who would put their hand in a fire and not listen to what their pain sensors were telling them: *Get it out!* Yet we often do not follow this natural reflex in many areas of our lives including relationships of various kinds.

In our attempts to avoid change, we start rationalizing and twisting the truth until reality becomes unrecognizable. This leads to self-doubt, which sets in motion a chain of events that creates undesired, if not disastrous and self-destructive results. There is no good substitute that I know of for taking right action at the right time, but that requires the courage to change. We must be sensitive to ourselves to understand the changes that are continually talking place not only in the outward expression of our creativity and the changing world around us, but also the changes taking place inside us, because we are creating those changes with our thoughts and resulting actions.

Another one of the great lessons of change that we are presented with is detachment, the ultimate *physical* aspect of this lesson is our having to eventually give up our own bodies in order to move freely into the next level of our experience of love and creativity. But we can even look at that eventuality as something quite beautiful: bidding farewell and thanks to our bodies for the loving service they gave to the evolution of our higher self. The *Bhagavad Gita* gives such calming reassurance concerning our ultimate expression of detachment in this life: think of it as a change of clothes.[86]

We can view our friendships and close personal relationships in the same metaphoric light: we feed them, try to keep them pure and healthy, appreciate all the beauty we can experience with them and through them, and also what we can learn from the pains. We must love, honor and nurture them. We lovingly offer spiritual service to one another through the purity of our thoughts, words, and actions, and in our quest for growth we bid one another farewell when it is time to move on to the new experiences that will help us to further evolve.

It is important to the evolution of our creativity to not fear change because ours is a continual journey of discovery and expansion. We must not get stuck traveling in the same monotonous circle, continually repeating the same patterns no matter how lovely a particular aspect of our creative expression may be or how popular it has become. Popularity can sometimes have a down side if we are not careful. If people particularly like something that we do, they understandably want us to stay in that place and continue repeating it over and over so they can continue to enjoy whatever it is they have become accustomed to and resonate with. When, for our own growth, we depart from that familiar pattern, it can sometimes upset and confuse them. But as long as we are changing, evolving for the right reasons, and we try to help people adjust to the changes in a caring and compassionate way, we help them to grow by exposing them to new levels of our creativity, in addition to the popular works we have done. It doesn't have to be one or the other. We don't have to "throw the baby out with the bathwater," as the saying goes. In a way, everyone wins from the experience if we allow change to unfold naturally.

As we evolve we are presented with new levels of opportunity to grow and must be alert to them and be ready to welcome those opportunities without fear or hesitation. If we are quiet enough internally to allow our intuitive magic and inner voice to guide us, then we will have no doubt about what to do when the answers we are searching for are spontaneously presented.

The opening words of the inspiring radio program *New Dimensions* tells us, "It is only through a change in human consciousness that the world will be transformed."[87] Our hearts must change. They must become softer and more tender, filled with compassion and understanding and the willingness to strive for peace and wholeness for all of creation. How that change of heart is brought about depends on each individual circumstance, but as long as pure love is the motivating force behind all our actions, we stand the best chance of succeeding no matter which designated path is best for each of us.

"It is never too late to become what you might have been."

George Eliot
English author and novelist

Change Quotations

Change Quotations

"Time is a dressmaker specializing in alterations."

Faith Baldwin
American novelist

"To exist is to change, to change is to mature, to mature is
to go on creating oneself endlessly."

Henri Bergson
French Philosopher

"There is nothing permanent except change."

Heraclitus
Greek philosopher

"Human beings, by changing the inner attitudes of their
minds, can change the outer aspects of their lives."

William James
American philosopher and psychologist

"Only in growth, reform, and change, paradoxically enough,
is true security to be found."

Anne Morrow Lindbergh
American writer

"How does one become a butterfly?" she asked pensively.
"You must want to fly so much that you are willing to give
up being a caterpillar."

Trina Paulus
American artist, sculptor, and author

"Everyone thinks of changing the world, but no one thinks
of changing himself."

Leo Tolstoy
Russian novelist and philosopher

"Your current safe boundaries were once unknown frontiers."

Unknown author

"The most powerful agent of growth and transformation is
something much more basic than any technique: a change
of heart."

John Welwood
American psychologist and author

Creativity and Gratitude

Chapter Fifteen
Creativity and Gratitude

*"If the only prayer you say in your whole life is
'thank you', that would suffice."*

Meister Eckhart
German Christian mystic

Living in a spirit of gratitude, no matter what our challenges may be, can help us to live in the moment, putting our attention on all the things we can be grateful for; being grateful for what we *do* have instead of focusing on what we do not have. Learning to keep our wants and desires from escalating to unhealthy levels gives us greater assurance that we will be able to maintain balance. It will also assist us in developing the necessary insight to be able to view the circumstances and realities of our lives with equanimity.

"When you are grateful, fear disappears and abundance appears."

Anthony Robbins

Sometimes our view of life gets so clouded by many of the problems, challenges, and disappointments that we all face, and we allow them to distort our picture of reality, sidetracking our attention from what is true. We block out the light that contains the energy and information that we need to live and create with clarity of mind and spirit. Once we lose that clarity, we can easily begin to fall into a negative spin, whose downward spiral becomes harder and harder from which to recover.

Despite our having many dreams and desires that may have yet to be fulfilled, we still have much to be grateful for. Often times it's just a matter of adjusting our perspective, as the following poetic and beautifully metaphoric words of French writer Alphonse Karr express: "Some people are always grumbling that roses have thorns; I am thankful that thorns have roses." If each of us took a few moments to make a list of our blessings, then perhaps our outlook would become brighter, and our hearts lighter. Actress and television personality Oprah Winfrey encourages us to "keep a grateful journal every night. List five things that you are grateful for." In doing so, we can begin each new day with a renewed spirit of hope and adventure about life and all the new and interesting things we can experience and learn from each magical moment we view the world through ageless eyes.

"Gratitude is the most exquisite form of courtesy."
Jacques Maritain

It is an expression of dignity, humility, and respect, to thoughtfully show our appreciation and gratitude to others and to our Higher Power, not just in words, but through our deeds. The late President John F. Kennedy stated, "As we express our gratitude, we must never forget that the highest appreciation is not to utter words, but to live by them." We must be living examples of what we believe. How we choose to live our lives will reflect just how much appreciation and gratitude we feel, not only toward others, but also toward ourselves.

One very important expression of gratitude is generosity. Our sincere willingness to show our gratitude through a generous and loving heart, is an accurate indicator of the true wealth and richness of our lives.

"They who give have all things; they who withhold have nothing."

Hindu proverb

We can dispel the clouds of darkness and despair of the world with the warm, illumined beams of loving gratitude and generosity, and "Be grateful for the joy of life. Be glad for the privilege of work. Be thankful for the opportunity to give and serve."[88] Let us be grateful for the privilege of being able to do all that we can to bring peace, goodness, and beauty to the world through the loving expression of our uniquely inspired creative gifts.

"Gratitude is the sign of noble souls."

Aesop
Greek writer

Gratitude Quotations

Gratitude Quotations

"Gratitude is the fairest blossom which springs from the soul."

Henry Ward Beecher
American preacher, speaker, and writer

"Gratitude is not only the greatest of virtues, but the parent of all the others."

Marcus Tullius Cicero
Roman orator, statesman, philosopher, and writer

"Water exposed to "Thank you" formed beautiful hexagonal crystals . . . The vibration of good words has a positive effect on the world . . ."[89]

Masaru Emoto
Japanese author and doctor of alternative medicine

"When one's expectations are reduced to zero, one really appreciates everything one does have."

Stephen Hawking
English physicist

"The deepest principle in human nature is the craving to be appreciated."

William James
American Philosopher and psychologist

"A man of genius is unbearable, unless he possesses at least two things besides: gratitude and purity."

Friedrich Nietzsche
German philosopher

"We often take for granted the very things that most deserve our gratitude."

Cynthia Ozick
American novelist

"Nothing is more honorable than a grateful heart."

Seneca
Roman philosopher

"Feeling gratitude and not expressing it is like wrapping a present and not giving it."

William Arthur Ward
American college administrator

Creativity and Good Health

Chapter Sixteen
Creativity and Good Health

"If any organism fails to fulfill its potentialities, it becomes sick."
William James
American philosopher and psychologist

There exists within each of us an orchestra of different frequencies that creates the music of our bodies, the symphony of our soul. Those frequencies correspond to how we feel, creating harmony when we're well and happy, and dissonance when we are unhealthy and out of balance. We are either "in tune" or "out of tune" with ourselves and our surroundings, depending on our state of being. Our thoughts, emotions, and feelings are constantly being eavesdropped on by every cell. Each part of our body has a sound, a frequency, a kind of unique "theme" that is assigned accordingly to the various sections of our internal orchestra playing the composition of life within us. When played in tune, those themes help to create a powerfully magnetic performance full of energy and life. However, if one or more elements of the orchestra are playing out of tune, it affects the whole performance, compromising the overall beauty of the composition and influencing how it is ultimately received. It also affects the morale of the other sections of the orchestra. And the "audience," those seemingly outside of ourselves, can also tell that something is wrong, inharmonious, and out of tune.

There are people whose extrasensory perception allows them to actually *hear* illness in others. They can hear the sounds, the "music" other people are broadcasting, and are able to identify which section of the internal orchestra is playing out of tune. They can "hear" when someone has cancer or other diseases that change the normal frequency of a healthy person. They "sound" different. They are vibrating differently than someone who has good health. Some animals can even smell cancer and that too involves extrasensory sensitivity to very subtle vibrations, a more heightened olfactory sensitivity. According to an article on this subject, "Dogs have 40 times the number of scent-receiving cells in their noses than humans have, making them able to sense the most minute scents given off by tumor cells."[90] The article goes on to say that after a year and a half of training, a dog was right 87 percent of the time in detecting cancer in humans.

It's not hard to imagine that cancer or other diseases have their own sound or tuning that doesn't blend well with the rest of the internal orchestra. They create dissonance, which causes discomfort and a lack of harmony, which in turn causes an overall imbalance. It might be thought of as one section of the orchestra initiating a coup d'etat. The coup may or may not be ultimately successful, but in the interim, the performance will be disrupted. Once the offender has been either brought back in tune, or removed, harmony and balance can then be restored to the whole and the music of life can resume.

The body is the outward manifestation of the mind. It is the hardcopy, the readout of our thoughts, so our emotions play a very significant role in fashioning our physical state of being. If our emotions are kept bottled up, they search for an alternate pathway of expression, unfortunately very often finding it in the form of cancer and other diseases. Those pent up emotions can literally eat us alive. According to the wonderful work of Dr. Candace Pert, the immune cells are thinking cells that play a significant role in affecting mood and emotion.[91] And since our immune cells make the same chemicals our brain makes when we think, negative or repressed emotions can greatly compromise our immune system's ability to fight disease. She explains in her book, *The Molecules of Emotion*, that intelligence is not limited to the brain but is found everywhere in our body, and the stress created from repressed feelings and emotions cause blockages which create the conditions that lead to disease.[92]

I'm in complete agreement with Dr. Pert's statement that "all emotions are positive emotions," including anger and sadness, which to her, "are as healthy as peace, courage and joy."[93] Even fear, when based in truth, has its right time and place in serving to protect us from harm. Honestly, I am very wary of people who appear "positive" all the time. It's just not natural. Quite often I think the reality is actually more one of denial and buried emotions than that of being "positive." Problems occur, however, when emotions such as anger, sadness, and fear get out of control. Life is a big balancing act, and to be healthy, everything has to be balanced.

We have a spectrum of emotions for a good reason: *they're all valid*. They all play an important role in our overall health and healthy self-expression. They all serve an important purpose and must be allowed to flow freely. When our natural pathways of emotional expression become blocked and fail to function properly, the loss of energy, the depletion of our *prana*,[94] *chi*, or *lifeforce*, creates a mood of unhappiness, discontent, and imbalance. Happiness and good health are dependant upon each other because our emotions and physical well-being are inseparable. They are two sides of the same coin. So too, in order to allow our creativity to flow in healthy ways, we must also allow our emotions to flow freely.

Touch and body work can help open blocked pathways and release the unhealthy concentration of trapped energy. Yoga and meditation can also aid in our being re-energized, as can Tai Chi[95] and Chi Kung.[96] And the soothing music that is associated with these forms of relaxation helps to create a healing atmosphere. Getting into a healthy routine of exercise of some kind is always recommended in trying to restore balance to our bodymind. And something as simple as just taking a walk in a natural setting can work its own miracles in helping us to regain a state of wellness and peace.

One amazingly simple thing that helped me during my recovery from the earlier mentioned near-death experience I had, came from the wisdom of the Native American Medicine Cards[97] that a friend, a wise old sage of a woman, kindly read to me. It consisted of just lying on the grass, in the tranquil park that I love, letting the energy of the earth's healing vibrations realign every cell back to perfect balance. When I tried the same thing just standing barefoot on the grass, I felt a cool beam of energy go right through me from bottom to top, and upon reaching the top, that beam of energy never failed to literally move the muscles of my face, forming a big smile that wouldn't quit. And believe it or not, even *hugging a tree* can help us reconnect with the Earth's natural vibration and re-establish equilibrium and good health. I'm not ashamed to say that I've done it many times. I think of trees as loving beings, loving friends whose unconditional love is a great comfort.

We must create a safe and healthy environment for ourselves, a sacred place somewhere in our world within which we can feel free to express our uncensored creative truth without fear of judgment. As we gain confidence in ourselves, and confidence in the outward expressions of our creative mind, we can then expand that sacred space to encompass the whole world by our having manifested around us an aura of immunity to the negative thoughts and opinions of others. The only thing our awareness will be focused on, the only thing that will matter, is our truth, because that truth will not only insure our own good health and happiness, it will ultimately help heal the world.

"Health is the greatest of all possessions."
Isaac Bickerstaff
Irish playwright

Health Quotations

Health Quotations

"Feelings are energy. Repressed feelings are blocked energy.
We don't do our best when we are blocked."

Melody Beattie
American author

"Emotion always has its roots in the unconscious and
manifests itself in the body."

Irene Claremont de Castillejo
Jungian psychologist

"In a disordered mind, as in a disordered body, soundness
of health is impossible."

Marcus Tullius Cicero
Roman orator, statesman, philosopher, and writer

"True friendship is like sound health, the value of it is seldom
known until it be lost."

Charles Colton
English clergyman and writer

"It is no measure of health to be well adjusted to a profoundly sick society."

J. Krishnamurti
Indian mystic

"Love cures people—both the ones who give it and the ones who receive it."

Dr. Karl Menninger
American psychiatrist and author

"Sickness is the vengeance of nature for the violation of her laws."

Charles Simmons
American writer

"Health is a state of complete physical, mental and social well-being, and not merely the absence of disease or infirmity."

World Health Organization, 1948

"Doing good to others is not a duty. It is a joy, for it increases your own health and happiness."

Zoraster
Religious prophet and founder of Zoroastrianism

Creativity and Success

Chapter Seventeen
Creativity and Success

"Success is a journey not a destination."

Arthur Ashe
American tennis champion

The meaning of success may be different to different people. It can be as subjective and as personal as what each person's idea of beauty is. But perhaps the real meaning of success is something that each of us must search our souls for and discover for ourselves.

Success doesn't necessarily have much to do with money, although money can be part of it. We must not confuse the dollar value placed on something with its *true* value. Money is something we receive in exchange for the service we offer. No need to apologize for that. But perhaps success has more to do with an inner feeling of happiness and peace and a sense of personal and creative accomplishment rather than what society dictates it is. In fact I have the feeling that what society usually sells as success, with the amassing of material wealth and the social pretensions that often go hand in hand with it, is a good indication of what *true* success *is not*. It's a much more soulful experience than that. It can include wealth of various kinds but is not limited to any one of them. In the words of American writer Elbert Hubbard,

"The secret of success is this: there is no secret of success." It is a natural consequence of living our creative truth.

If we do what we love and love what we do, we stand the best chance of succeeding. But so many people are afraid of doing what they love, really *going for it*, because they are afraid of failing in the process of trying. The ironic thing, though, is that if we don't try, then we have already failed. By not at least trying our very best to develop our gifts to their full potential, we lose the golden opportunity to share all the goodness we could have brought to the world; we fail to live the life that was intended by our Higher Power, one of abundance, generosity, happiness, peace, and love. However, "in every failure is the seed of success."[98] So, if we do fall short of what we are capable of, we can acknowledge this with dignity and honesty and allow the experience to help us to better ourselves. But we can only do so by truly learning from our mistakes, not repeating them, and then closing the book and moving on.

We can never be considered a failure if we have tried our best, and a quote by Scottish journalist B.C. Forbes, attests to this truth: "The man who has done his level best . . . is a success, even though the world may write him down as a failure." All of the things discussed in this book can help us to live and create successfully: love, honesty, good health, good self-esteem, right living, courage, commitment, a willingness to change, as well as humility, gratitude, compassion, forgiveness, and a joyful spirit. Following these signposts along life's path will help insure that no matter what our circumstances may be, we will be successful in our noble pursuits.

If we were to leave this life today, would we feel a sense of accomplishment and fulfillment? Would we feel closure? Being a part of the infinite cosmos, our potential is also infinite, yet this life is so short. Considering this reality, one might feel that he or she could have accomplished so much more. But in light of the time we are given here, whether it's one year or one-hundred years, did we make the very best of that time? Could we leave with our hearts and minds at peace knowing that we had done well not only for ourselves but also in behalf of others? Would we feel we left something creative that was a reflection of the beauty of our souls, whether it be a child or a composition or a garden? Did we make others happy as well as ourselves? Did our being here make a positive difference in the lives of others? If we can answer "yes" to that last question alone, then I believe we succeeded brilliantly on our journey of love and have embraced the spirit of creativity.

"The road to success is always under construction."
Paul Harvey
American radio broadcaster

Success Quotations

Success Quotations

"The ability to convert ideas to things is the secret of outward success."

Henry Ward Beecher
American preacher, speaker, and writer

"Shoot for the moon. Even if you miss, you'll land among the stars."

Les Brown
American motivational speaker

"Success is following the pattern of life one enjoys most."

Al Capp
American cartoonist

"One secret of success in life is for a man to be ready for his opportunity when it comes."

Benjamin Disraeli
Former Prime Minister of the United Kingdom

"He is considered successful in our day who gets more out of life than he puts in. But a man of value will give more than he receives."

Albert Einstein
German-born American physicist

"Don't aim for success if you want it; just do what you love and believe in, and it will come naturally."

David Frost
British television journalist

"Prosperity is living easily and happily in the real world, whether you have money or not."

Jerry Gillies
American author and speaker

"A man's true wealth is the good he does in the world."

Mohammed
Religious prophet and founder of Islam

"The biggest block to any man's success is in his head."

Unknown Author

"Persistence may be the key to success, but the key to failure . . . is trying to please everybody."

Unknown Author

Some Final Thoughts

Chapter Eighteen
Some Final Thoughts

"To love a person
is to learn the song in their heart,
and sing it to them when they have forgotten."

Anonymous

A creative life is for all of us, but our creativity must be developed, exercised, and put to good use. It must be nurtured and our creative muscles must be flexed or else complacency-induced atrophy sets in. As part of the gift of life, we have a responsibility to create. It is up to each of us to express our infinite creativity to the very best of our ability, in the most positive and uplifting ways. How we use our creative powers is of great importance. If motivated by the wrong intentions, creative energy can be directed in harmful ways. Just look at all the sophisticated weapons that have been created with the intent to cause maximum pain, suffering, and devastation. I remember trying to speak to a man about peace, who proudly countered that he designed "systems that destroy people." This is obviously not an honorable way of utilizing one's creativity. Therefore educating people about the nature and source of their true creativity can help insure that the form of creative expression will be healthy and helpful to others instead of destructive and hurtful. Our creative expression and the fruit it bears must be based upon love, with the intention of creating loving results for the greater good.

The good we do continues to live on far past this lifetime, echoing throughout the universe and beyond in ways that we may not be able to comprehend right now. But be assured that it does. When we feel that our good works go unnoticed or unappreciated, we must keep in mind that nothing is lost. Our love and goodness, right from the moment of creation, help bring about great transformations, not only here, but everywhere.

No matter what I have been able to accomplish in my own very short lifetime so far, I know that I will not even begin to scratch the surface of my potential, so I must let go of my attachment to all of that and just do what I love to do for that reason alone. I believe the universe will take care of the rest at the right time. This is where our faith often gets tested, not by something or someone outside of ourselves, but by our own level of commitment.

We have a partnership with the universe. We're in business with the universe. If we do our share, the universe will take care of its share, making sure that what we have to offer is properly distributed in the proper way at the proper time. Just do what you love to do, with all the love you have to give, from wherever you are, and leave the rest to the grand orchestration of the universe. Author Deepak Chopra expressed so beautifully that "Each of us has a 'dharma,' a purpose in life. When we are in dharma we enjoy and love our work. Whatever service we are here to give there is a demand for it. Create and foresee that demand for which you have come here and offer that demand and the supply is guaranteed."[99]

Writing this book with a spirit of love actually helped me to endure and overcome many of the personal and professional challenges that I was facing during the period of its creation. I feel that this book was a gift given to me as a model to follow so that I too may better learn the lessons that will help me to evolve spiritually and creatively. It was an answer to so many of my prayers about how to understand and overcome my own challenges. So, once again, I feel that I have not been the source, but a channel for the goodness in the information that has hopefully been presented here. Through the loving spirit of trying to help others, I have become the greatest recipient of the very goodness that I had hoped to help others achieve in finding and living the true spirit of creativity.

> "The future belongs to those who believe in the beauty of their dreams."
>
> Eleanor Roosevelt
> American social activist and stateswoman

Being I

I'm learning about the tree that I am
and the wind that I am,
the birds and the bees that I am.
I am we, we are they, they are me
dancing in chaotic synchronicity,
each pirouette perfectly planned,
the choreographer holding the moves
in His hand . . .
But I am that too.
I am He, He is me
playing hide and seek,
trying to keep myself amused,
pretending that I don't
but know the rules.
Creating lifetimes in a wisp,
being all I hope to be,
connecting dots across the sky
in my mind's eye.
I breathe when the seasons do,
catch the angle of their shadow and hue,
embrace the sad November dusk
and hold it's light to my heavy heart.

I come from somewhere long ago,
whereabouts unknown . . .
But somewhere beyond the patch of blue,
deep in the heart of you,
that's where you'll find me.

Joseph Curiale
1995

End Notes

1   http://www.peopleinspirit.com/poems___quotes_of_remembrance.html

2   http://home.comcast.net/~garbl/stylemanual/c.htm

3   http://hem.passagen.se/xjonken/creativity.html

4   http://www.m-w.com/cgi-bin/ dictionary?book=Dictionary&va
=create&x=0&y=0

5   M. Talbot, *The Holographic Universe* (New York: HarperPerennial, 1991) pp.16-17

6   Ibid., pp. 54

7   D. Chopra, *What is the Nature of Reality*, A Talk Given by Dr. Deepak Chopra, M.D. at the Seattle Center on May 18, 1991. Originally appeared in Vol. 1, No. 21 of The Sovereign Scribe, P.O. Box 350, McKenna, WA 98558 http://www.ascension-research.org/reality.html

8   A. Watts, *The Relevance of Oriental Philosophy*, A lecture given by Alan Watts in 1973, transcribed by Charles Kluepfel, http://members aol.com/chasklu/religion/private/watts.htm

9   http://whatis.techtarget.com/definition/0, sid9_gci554508,00.html

10   10. D. Chopra, *What is the Nature of Reality*, A Talk Given by Dr. Deepak Chopra, M.D. at the Seattle Center on May 18, 1991. Originally appeared in Vol. 1, No. 21 of The Sovereign Scribe,

P.O. Box 350, McKenna, WA 98558 http://www.ascension-research.org/reality.html

[11] A. Watts, *The Relevance of Oriental Philosophy*, A lecture given by Alan Watts in 1973, transcribed by Charles Kluepfel, http://members.aol.com/chasklu/religion/private/watts.htm

[12] 1 John 4:8 *The Blue Letter Bible*, http://www.blueletterbible.org/1Jo/1Jo004.html

[13] http://deoxy.org/w_nature.htm

[14] D. Bohm, *On Creativity* (New York, London: Routeledge, 2004) pg. 20

[15] Ibid., pg. 3

[16] H. Khan, *The Mysticism of Sound and Music* (Boston: Shambala Publications, 1991), pg. 101

[17] John 8:32, *The Bible (New Living translation) http://bible.gospelcom.net/passage/?search=John%208:32;&version=51;*

[18] G. Kneller, *The Art and Science of Creativity* (New York: Holt, Rinehard and Winston) 1965

[19] M. Whiteside, *The Journal of Creative Behavior*, Vol. 15 Number 3, (Buffalo: The Creative Education Foundation, 1981) pg. 197

[20] M. Emoto, *The Hidden Messages in Water* (Oregon: Beyond Words Publishing, 2004) pg. 98

[21] http://www.halexandria.org/dward428.htm

[22] http://www.crystalinks.com/reincarnation2.html

[23] S. Hawking, *The Theory of Everything* (Beverly Hills: New Millennium Press, 2003) pg. 92-93

[24] http://www.spiritsite.com/writing/deecho/part37.shtml

[25] http://www.annieappleseedproject.org/deepchoponql.html

[26] B. Franklin, "I look upon death to be as necessary to the constitution as sleep. We shall rise refreshed in the morning." And, "Finding myself to exist in the world, I believe I shall, in some shape or other always exist."

J. London, "I did not begin when I was born, nor when I was conceived. I have been growing, developing, through incalculable myriads of millenniums. All my previous selves have their voices, echoes, promptings in me. Oh, incalculable times again shall I be born."

M. Twain, "I have been born more times than anybody except Krishna."

L. Tolstoy, "As we live through thousands of dreams in our present life, so is our present life many thousands of such lives which we enter from the other more real life and then return after death. Our life is but one of the dreams of that more real life, and so it is endlessly, until the very last one, the very real the life of God."

H. Ford, "I adopted the theory of reincarnation when I was 26. Genius is experience. Some think to seem that it is a gift or talent, but it is the fruit of long experience in many lives."

W. Whitman, "I know I am deathless. No doubt I have died myself ten thousand times before. I laugh at what you call dissolution, and I know the amplitude of time."

G.S. Patton, "So as through a glass and darkly, the age long strife I see, where I fought in many guises, many names, but always me."

W. Wordsworth, "Our birth is but a sleep and a forgetting; The Soul that rises with us, our life's Star, Hath had elsewhere its setting. And cometh from afar."

Socrates, "I am confident that there truly is such a thing as living again, that the living spring from the dead, and that the souls of the dead are in existence."

R.W. Emerson, "The soul comes from without into the human body, as into a temporary abode, and it goes out of it anew it passes into other habitations, for the soul is immortal." "It is the secret of the world that all things subsist and do not die, but only retire a little from sight and afterwards return again. Nothing is dead; men feign themselves dead, and endure mock funerals... and there they stand looking out of the window, sound and well, in some strange new disguise."

H.D. Thoreau, "Why should we be startled by death? Life is a constant putting off of the mortal coil - coat, cuticle, flesh and bones, all old clothes."

[27] http://www.skepticsannotatedbible.com/mt/17.html

[28] M. Whiteside, *The Journal of Creative Behavior*, Vol. 15 Number 3, (Buffalo: The Creative Education Foundation, 1981) pg. 197

[29] http://www.virtualpet.com/vp/farm/petrock/petrock.htm

[30] R. May, *The Courage to Create* (New York: W.W. Norton & Company 1994)

[31] http://www.astronomy.com/ASY/CS/forums/267110/ShowPost.aspx

[32] M. Emoto, *The Hidden Messages in Water* (Oregon: Beyond Words Publishing, 2004) pg. xxii

[33] G. Kinnell

[34] Edward O. Wilson, American Scientist (1929-)

[35] J. Arguelles, *The Transformative Vision* (Boston: Shambala Publications, 1975)

[36] M. Toms, *Fritjof Capra in Conversation with Michael Toms (New Dimensions Books)*, (Lower Lake: Aslan 1994) pg. 72

[37] G. Zukav, *The Dancing Wu Li Masters* (London: Penguin Group, 1993) pg. 8

[38] http://www.watchtower.org/library/w/2003/7/1/article_02.htm

[39] Ibid.

[40] D. Chopra, *Creating Affluence* (Audio), (San Raphael: Amber- Allen Publishing, 2003)

[41] T. Kooser, *The Poetry Home Repair Manual* (Lincoln and London: University of Nebraska Press 2005) pg. 2

[42] Talbot, M., *Mysticism and the New Physics* (New York: HarperPerennial, 1992) pg. 3

[43] Ibid.

[44] H. Khan, *The Mysticism of Sound and Music* (Boston: Shambala Publications, 1991) pg. 15, 29-30

[45] A. Watts, *The Book*, (Toronto, Vintage 1989)

[46] M. Emoto, *The Hidden Messages in Water* (Oregon: Beyond Words Publishing, 2004) pg. 48

[47] H. Khan, *The Mysticism of Sound and Music* (Boston: Shambala Publications, 1991) pg. 101

[48] G. Cooper, and B. Henderson, *Leap of Faith* (New York: HarperCollins, 2000) pg. 244

[49] http://www.feb.se/EMFguru/Elf/tribune/lacrosse.html

[50] G. Cooper, and B. Henderson, *Leap of Faith* (New York: HarperCollins, 2000) pg. 244

[51] "The Faraday cage is an electrical apparatus designed to prevent the passage of electromagnetic waves, either containing them in or excluding them from its interior space. It is named for physicist Michael Faraday, who built the first one in 1836." http://en.wikipedia.org/wiki/Faraday_cage

[52] G. Cooper, and B. Henderson, *Leap of Faith* (New York: HarperCollins, 2000) pg. 243

[53] 6. Ibid. pg. 242

[54] Ibid. Pg. 245

[55] D. Chopra, *The New Physics of Healing* (Audio), (Boulder: Sounds True 2002)

[56] D. Chopra, *The New Physics of Healing* (Audio), (Boulder: Sounds True 2002)

[57] E.P. Torrance, and L.K. Hall, *The Journal of Creative Behavior*, Vol. 14 Number 1, Buffalo, The Creative Education Foundation, 1980

[58] http://movies2.nytimes.com/gst/movies/movie.html?v_id=135717

[59] http://wordnet.princeton.edu/perl/webwn?s=truth

[60] Encarta World Dictionary as part of Microsoft Word

[61] Ibid.

[62] http://www.thefreedictionary.com/truth

[63] http://www.globalspirituality.info/knowledge/#truth

[64] http://www.m-w.com/cgi-bin/dictionary?book=Dictionary&va=truth

[65] http://www.thefreedictionary.com/truth

[66] http://www.freesearch.co.uk/dictionary/truth

[67] D. Chopra, *The New Physics of Healing* (Audio), (Boulder: Sounds True 2002)

[68] B. Marciniak, *Bringers of the Dawn* (Santa Fe New Mexico: Bear and Company, 1992) pg. 212

[69] Ibid. pg. 219

[70] M. Emoto, *The Hidden Messages in Water* (Oregon: Beyond Words Publishing, 2004) pg. xxvii

[71] R. May, *The Courage to Create* (New York: W.W. Norton & Company 1994) pg. 21

[72] M. Emoto, *The Hidden Messages in Water* (Oregon: Beyond Words Publishing, 2004) pg. 142

[73] M. Whiteside, *The Journal of Creative Behavior*, Vol. 15 Number 3, (Buffalo: The Creative Education Foundation, 1981) pg. 192

[74] Luke 14:28 *The New American Standard Bible*, http://bible.gospelcom. net/passage/?search=luke%2014;&version=49;

[75] Sai Baba, *Sathya Sai Speaks Vol. 15* (Prashanti Nilayam: Sri Sathya Sai Books and Publications Trust, 1982)

[76] S. Hawking, *The Theory of Everything* (Beverly Hills: New Millennium Press, 2003) pg. 9

[77] Black Elk, J. Neihardt, *Black Elk Speaks* (Lincoln/London: University of Nebraska Press, 21st Century Edition, 2000)

[78] H. Smith, The *Wisdom of Huston Smith* (Audio) (San Francisco: New Dimensions Radio)

[79] R. Niebuhr

[80] M. Whiteside, *The Journal of Creative Behavior* Vol. 15 Number 3, (Buffalo: The Creative Education Foundation, 1981) pg. 195

[81] Luke 6:31, *The Bible*, (New International Reader's Version0 http://bible.gospelcom.net/passage/?search=luke%206:31;&version=76;

[82] D.J. Schwartz, *The Magic of Thinking Big* (New York, Simon and Schuster, Inc. 1987)

[83] M. Whiteside, *The Journal of Creative Behavior*, Vol. 15 Number 3, (Buffalo: The Creative Education Foundation, 1981) pg. 195

[84] Anonymous

[85] A. Watts, *Myth and Religion*, (Audio), (San Francisco: Electronic University)

[86] http://www.bhagavad-gita.us/introduction-to-bhagavad-gita.htm

[87] *New Dimensions Radio*, http://www.newdimensions.org/

[88] Grenville Kleiser

[89] M. Emoto, *The Hidden Messages in Water* (Oregon: Beyond Words Publishing, 2004) pg. xxv

[90] 1. http://www.jcrows.com/DogsBeingTrainedToSmellCancer.html

[91] C. Pert, *Molecules of Emotion* (New York: Touchstone, 1999)

[92] Ibid.

[93] Ibid.

[94] 5. *Prana*: "Prana is a Sanskrit word literally meaning 'life-force' the invisible bio-energy or vital energy that keeps the body alive and maintains a state of good health." Other names for this energy include, Ki (Japan), Chi (China), Pneuma (Greece), Mans (Polynesia), Ruah (Hebrew). http://www.crystalinks.com/pranic.html

[95] 6. *Tai Chi*, "also known as TAI CHI CH'UAN, and is part of the Tai Chi Ch'uan System, which, originally, was a formidable martial art operating on several levels of awareness. It embodies Taoist Philosophy, and accordingly is extremely beneficial to good health. Tai Chi is a comprehensive series of gentle physical movements, and breathing techniques, with mental and spiritual intent, which allows you to experience a meditative state. It is calming and rejuvenating, and assists the body and mind to maintain balance, and exercises the body, mind and spirit, together with the internal organs. It includes both the inner and outer expressions of the body and mind. Here we are able to balance the Yin and Yang life force energy of Chi. In this way this system develops the ability to balance the "yielding and attacking" aspects in martial art combat. It has also been such a major influence in all the martial arts we see today." http://healersoftheworld.com/glossary/glossaryR-U.html#taichi

[96] 7. *Chi Kung*, "or "Energy Control," dates back to over 4,000 years, and is the art of developing and utilizing universal energy that is necessary for good health, vitality, mind expansion and spiritual development. It is the sacred art of self-healing through the practice and experience of working and being the life force energy. There are many varieties and different forms of this powerful form of self-healing, and raising of consciousness, which are an integral part of Chinese medicine, even to this day. Being such an ancient practice, it was developed in the monasteries, and was a major contributor to a number of the martial arts of today. It is a means by which one can balance the Qi, or Chi, or Life Force Energy, within the body, mind and spirit, to attain and maintain good health, calmness, and raise consciousness. It can be seen as meditation in motion, using postures, physical movements, and breathing, all in a very gentle fashion. When the Qi is developed remarkable things

happen. You only have to read about the Qi Gong Masters, of whom such a guiding light, is Yan Xin, and many others. Their abilities and healing attributes are phenomenal." http:// healersoftheworld.com/glossary/glossaryA-D.html#chikung

[97] *Medicine Cards*: "Unlike the meaning that we have come to recognize for "medicine"... Native Americans define it as a way of life where one walks in perfect harmony with the Universe bringing healing to everyone and thing that one comes in contact with. Medicine cards are designed to teach . . . life lessons by empowering . . . with the wisdom, lesson, spirit, and strength of a Native American animal. This is done so that the client may both have victory over his current situation, and reciprocate by giving back to Mother Earth. In this manner he fulfills his duty and place in the Great Mystery (life)." http://www.aatarot. com/readings/medicine.htm

[98] D. Chopra, *Creating Affluence* (Audio), (San Raphael: Amber- Allen Publishing, 2003)

[99] D. Chopra, *Creating Affluence* (Audio), (San Raphael: Amber- Allen Publishing, 2003)

Bibliography

Arguelles, J., *The Transformative Vision*. Boston: Shambhala, 1975

Barron, F., *Creative Person and the Creative Process*. New York: Holt, Rinehart and Winston 1969

Beattie, M., *Co-Dependent No More*. Minnesota: Hazeldon, 1992

Bohm, D., *On Creativity*. London, New York: Routeledge, 2004

Chopra, D., *Creating Affluence*. San Raphael: Amber—Allen Publishing, 2003

Chopra, D., *Magical Mind Magical Body* (Audio). New York: Simon & Shuster Audio 2003

Chopra, D., *The New Physics of Healing*. (Audio), Boulder: Sounds True 2002

Chopra, D., *The Spontaneous Fulfillment of Desires*, (Audio), New York, Random House 2003

Cooper, G., and Henderson, B., *Leap of Faith*. New York: HarperCollins, 2000

Emoto, M., *The Hidden Messages in Water*. Oregon: Beyond Words Publishing, 2004

Feng, G., and English, J., Tao *Te Ching, Lao Tsu*. New York: Vintage 1997

Hawking, S., *The Theory of Everything*. Beverly Hills: New Millennium Press, 2003

Hoffman, I., *The Tao Of Love*. New York: Prima Lifestyles, 1992

James, W., *The Principles of Psychology*. Cambridge: Harvard University Press, 1991

Khan, H., *The Mysticism of Sound and Music*. Boston: Shambala Publications, 1991

Kneller, G., *The Art and Science of Creativity*. New York: Holt Reinhart and Winston 1965

Kooser, T., *The Poetry Home Repair Manual*. Lincoln and London: University of Nebraska Press 2005

Krishnamurti, J., *Think on These Things*. New York: HarperPerennial 1989

Maltz, M., *Psycho-Cybernetics*. New York: Pocket; Reprint Edition, 1989

Marciniak, B., *Bringers of the Dawn*. Santa Fe New Mexico: Bear and Company, 1992

Marciniak, B., *The Path of Empowerment*. Maui: Inner Ocean Publishing 2004

May, R., *The Courage to Create*. New York: W.W. Norton & Company 1994

Mitchell E., Dr. *The Way of the Explorer*. New York: Putnam Adult, 1996

Paulus, T., *Hope for Flowers*. Mahwah, New Jersey: Paulist Press 1973

Pert, C., *Molecules of Emotion*. New York: Touchstone, 1999

Sai Baba, *Sathya Sai Speaks, Vol. 15*. Prashanti Nilayam: Sri Sathya Sai Books and Publications Trust, 1982

Schwartz, D., *The Magic of Thinking Big*. New York: Simon and Schuster, Inc. 1987

Shinn, F., *The Wisdom of Florence Scovel Shinn*. New York: Fireside 1989

Smith, H. *The Wisdom of Huston Smith*. (Audio) San Francisco: New Dimensions Radio

Talbot, M., *The Holographic Universe*. New York: HarperPerennial, 1991

Talbot, M., *Mysticism and the New Physics*. New York: HarperPerennial, 1992

Tharp, T., *The Creative Habit*, New York: Simon and Schuster, 2003

Thoreau, H.D., *Walden*. New York: Koneman 1996

Toms, M., *Fritjof Capra in Conversation with Michael Toms (New Dimensions Books)*. Lower Lake: Aslan 1994

Torrance, E.P., and Hall, L.K., *The Journal of Creative Behavior*. Vol. 14 Number 1, Buffalo: The Creative Education Foundation, 1980

Watts, A., *The Book*. Toronto: Vintage 1989

Watts, A., *Myth and Religion*, (Audio). San Francisco: Electronic University

Watts, A., *Philosophies of Asia*, (Audio). San Francisco: Electronic University

Whiteside, M., *The Journal of Creative Behavior*. Vol. 15 Number 3, Buffalo: The Creative Education Foundation, 1981

Yogananda, P., *Autobiography of a Yogi*. Los Angeles: Self-Realization Fellowship, 2003

Zukav, G., *The Dancing Wu Li Masters*. London: Penguin Group, 1993

About the Author

Composer and author Joseph Curiale has been described as "the poster boy for dreams come true." Arriving in Los Angeles in 1980 with nothing more than a passion for music and an unshakable belief in himself, he was writing music for The Tonight Show by 1982 and soon after became the first staff songwriter in the history of Columbia Pictures. He has composed and orchestrated music for movies, TV, and live performances, including Steve Martin's *Roxanne*. Among the television themes he has composed is the theme song for the long running, Emmy Award winning children's program, *Nick News*. His work on the soundtrack for the movie *Breakin'* sold over 4 million copies, while his orchestrations for *A Tribute To Sammy Davis Jr.* earned him an Emmy nomination. His compositions and arrangements have been recorded or performed by more than one hundred artists ranging from Janet and Michael Jackson to Kathleen Battle.

A near-death experience in Singapore in 1994 inspired Mr. Curiale to pursue his dreams of a life in concert music, to be able to express his musical soul freely without the limiting parameters of commercial music. He has since released two original CDs on the Orchard Road label, *Awakening* and *The Music Of Life*. Recorded with the London Symphony Orchestra, the Royal Philharmonic Orchestra, and Academy of Saint Martin in the Fields, they feature soloists including Doc Severinsen and some of the finest musicians from China and Japan. His music is often showcased on National Public Radio as well as in concert band, marching band, and symphonic performances. Reviewer Kevin Sutton has described Mr. Curiale as "a composer who is serious about his beliefs, deep in his thoughts and emotions . . . . He says what he means and means what he says, and is refreshingly unabashed about his desire to create beauty, and in his efforts to uplift the human state." A deeply spiritual man, his works are recognized the world over for their passion, beauty and sense of wonder.

A true Renaissance Man who is creative to the core, Joseph Curiale is an accomplished writer, poet, photographer, artist, and educator, whose book *The Spirit of Creativity*, is an insightful, passionate, and inspiring guide to exploring, unlocking, and honoring the creative spirit in everyone.

www.josephcuriale.com